The Secret Diary of a Seer

Happy, Sad, Joy, Bliss, Ecstasies of the Pleasure of Loving Jesus

by

JANE SCHROEDER

Contents

Dedication

This book is dedicated to my dearest, most cherished, beautiful mother, and granny to my children,
Agnes Jones,
one of the cloud of witnesses, whose visitations have sustained me on many occasions.
Also to my precious daughter and best friend,
Ruth Jemimah Merryweather

Special Thanks Go To

The most inspiring people in my life, my kids. Sam, always saying I can do it! Daughter, Ruth, from the day you were born I held you in my arms - you are beautiful inside and out!

Nigel Jones, my brother and accountant.

Pastor David Combs, Chester City Mission.

Ann Speed, family friend. Eileen Lea, lifelong family friend.   Rona Scot, my dear friend from Olive Branch. Elaine Hood, who shows me unconditional love. Justin & Rachael Abraham, Company of Burning Hearts.

Rebecca Morris, Artist.

Ian Clayton, Rabbi-Abba. Stephen McKie, buddy. Sally and Andy, tech support, and many other blessed people who have graced and enriched my life.

Introduction

My daughter, who is my biggest support, has always encouraged me to take the risk of saying it like it is, but still I have been hesitant about how vulnerable to be in this diary.

Tonight, on the way home from a hospital check-up, I was listening to a podcast by Ian Clayton where he was discussing his new book. I was so encouraged by the raw honesty of his work as I listened to him, it cemented in my mind that this diary will tell the highs and the lows of the life of a seer.

This compilation of stories and my life journey, from some of my diaries as far back as my childhood up to 2019, shows my spiritual journey intertwined from way back then and you will see and hear things coming through from my personal experiences, sometimes shared with family, friends and other people I have done life with, met and travelled within this exciting, sometimes crazy, but always beautiful walk with Yahweh, (I am constantly experiencing new things, gaining insight through the written Word and Living Word - Yeshua, the lover of my soul and heart's desire) and maturing under the influence of those I look up to and the ever-increasing guidance of the three in one God-head, Father, Son and Holy Spirit's union. I have been asked and told many times that the verbal accounts of my whacky experiences have helped others to accept that the wonderfully and sometimes seemingly crazy spiritual visions, experiences and manifestations are actually quite alright!

The support and grounding from leaders who are able to bring
the plumbline of Yahweh's word through Scripture has been a constant rudder in a sometimes stormy sea of opinion. I thank and honour those men and women of God in my life. The real person who set me on my life path was my pastor, Dr David Combs from Chester City Mission. He loved me, no matter what I did, even when I was really bad. He loved me through everything in my teens, teaching me to never forget the scripture, *John 3:16 "For God so loved the world he gave his only son, that whosoever believes in me shall not perish but have eternal life."*

I was praying one day when I saw, in a vision, a leaflet blowing right in front of my eyes. It was a piece of paper with a picture of the book cover; 3 trees depicting autumn, winter and summer.
I asked the Lord what this piece of paper was and heard clearly, "The Secret Diary of a Seer".

I said, "I don't think so, Lord. I am not the best communicator" and then proceeded to say all the other reasons which disqualified me from writing a book. I couldn't read till I was twelve years old, many years later discovering I had dyslexia when my son was diagnosed with it.

The very same year I saw the flyer to this book in the realms of the Kingdom of heaven, I met Chris Blackeby from Adelaide Australia. He asked if I was Jane Schroeder. I said yes and started crying. Chris said he felt I would write about seeing in heaven, indicating he was himself a publisher and would love to publish my books one day. He asked for some of my CD's. I sent him *Nun on the Run, The Seer Realm and The Pleasures of Loving Jesus.* My favourite all time message and the last of the CD's is called *Visitation* where I talk about how I saw into heaven. This CD doesn't sell but if people knew, they would be amazed as it teaches how to engage with the angelic.

Chris would continue to message me now and then asking how I was and how the book was coming on. I would write back, "It's not, because I'm too scared to do it!" It wasn't that I didn't think the book would be interesting, but I was just very insecure about people seeing who I really am.

A few years previous to the vision of the book cover a good friend and ministry partner suggested I write a few short stories about my experiences. He said that he thought I might write six or seven books and as he said it, I saw the colours of the different book covers. Oh, they will be growing like an orchard. I then simply put it out of my mind thinking, "Too hard." About a year before I started writing this book people kept giving me prophetic words saying I would write a book, seeing me writing books and books and books.

In 2018 I went to Australia and met Carol Foster who talked about writing books. I gave my usual excuses about growing up with dyslexia and not having enough time. We decided to face-time to talk about stories I might like to include in the book and as we talked, Carol would scribe the stories. We started at six am Australia time so she could get to the beach after the session before the sun got too strong. Surf's up baby!

I can't forget my bunny hunny Mexican mummy as I call her. Pearl Nagy, from Glory Company and I do girly time and encourage each other a lot with little messages. She would just seem to know when I needed encouragement. We are so connected in the heart. She was the first person to take me into Zion, the realms of the Kingdom. I was praying and went up into the mountains and there was a woman, a bit higher than me, on a mountain with long, black, gleaming, shiny hair wearing a long rusty-brown coloured suede skirt. As I met her, she pulled up a little of her skirt to reveal some cow hide boots cascading with brown suede fringe. She took me by the right hand and pulled me on a grey cloud to her level, platform. Pearl was on a mountain but on a cloud formation and from where we were seated, we could see Mount Zion with red kites flying around over to the top. I know we were watching interceding. It says in Psalms we are the Guidance of the earth.

Often, as I was praying in different seasons of my life, Pearl and I would be up there praying together. Just clouds with no sun and no blue sky.

I have seen myself with a tall Native American Indian many times discovering, as he walks the earth as an ever-living person appearing to other people, that like Enoch, he didn't die. This is significant to me as I have generational ties of native Canadian Indian down from my mum's side of the family. How wonderful is that! Partnering with heaven's council.

Foreword

Jane's pure heart, fierce tenacity and wide-eyed wonder for Jesus have granted her rich access into realms of the Kingdom where secrets and mysteries dwell. Through years of faithfulness, pioneering to push back religious limitations, Jane now invites us through her writings to go on a journey of awakening and step into these encounters.

Emma McKie

Jane Schroeder is a true Kingdom renaissance woman. What I love most about her is her glorious disregard of man's opinions when God has spoken. This book is so refreshing and alive, resonating with God's presence as Jane takes us on the journey of encounter. Prepare to be pushed and accelerated through reading this fresh revelation.

Teresa Bowen: Depths of Zion; Author of Zadok The New Old Order & The Fourth Wheel Story

I thank You, Lord, that I have this opportunity to say a few words about Jane's new book. The subject matter is 'seer', and that is something that has been a difficult walk with Jane. It was 40 years ago that she met me and we have walked this through together with the understanding of what God was saying and what God was doing, and how she would walk through this with the help of the Lord. So, I just want to say about this book, that it is one that needs to be heard. It needs to be spread across

England to Wales, Scotland and Northern Ireland, but my feeling is that it needs to go much further. It hasn't always been easy for the seers in this land.

Sometimes people can make comments like, "This is a little bit wild. This is something that is a fantasy or it's not true!" There are all sorts of statements that have been said over the years, but the reality is that the seer sees, and you will find when you read this book that Jane sees very clearly what God is doing, what God is saying and what He's saying to you and me and anybody else who reads this book.

So, if you read this book, you're going to really be blessed. It's a real privilege to be able to read it. I ask that you will read it and just pass it on to other seers who may be struggling. I thank You Lord for all that You have done to bring Jane to a maturity that's grown and grown and grown and it's been a privilege on my part to watch this happen, so I thank You Lord for all that You've done for her over these years. In Jesus Name, I say this.

Rona Scott

CHAPTER ONE

Angelic Hosts

I love when Angels engage with us. After having a dark supernatural childhood and suffering with fear, having such dynamic angelic encounters has filled my life with joy, assurance, peace and exciting, lasting experiences. I hope you are encouraged by my stories of angels, to open up, ask for and expect the supernatural visitation and appearance of angels.

Angels are created beings.
Colossians 1:16 (NASB) "For by Him, all things were created in heaven and on earth. The visible and the invisible, whether thrones or dominions or rulers or authorities."

Some angels minister to God. *Psalm 148:2 (PTP) "Go ahead praise him, all you Messengers! Praise him some more, all you heavenly hosts".*

Experiencing an Angel in Human Form
In April 2014, we were invited into the Capitol Building in Sacramento, California, by Shannon Grove, an Assembly member for the Thirty-Fourth Assembly District. While waiting for an opportunity to speak to Shannon amidst her busy schedule, my friend, Stevie McKie, and I decided to explore the magnificent spiral staircase leading to the most exquisite architecture in the building where we met a wonderful gentleman. The war veteran was in a wheelchair,

attending a meeting in honour of the Holocaust. Whilst there we had the privilege of viewing a blueprint room containing very large documents. They were the actual blueprints of the Capitol Building!

We moved on to the third floor where my attention was drawn to the window. As I looked out, I saw a beautiful rose garden, and decided to take a photograph of the view. I stood looking out of the window and I overheard a black African American woman standing nearby, talking on her pink flip-up mobile phone. She said, "The old transportation system won't get us where we need to go in the future." I stood nearer to her and gently touched her shoulder without thinking, saying out loud, "Thank you Jesus." She looked at me, smiled broadly and carried on talking on her mobile phone, then turned on her heels, pulling a black wheelie case, then walked towards the circular balcony staircase.

Stevie instantly felt to follow her, which he did, but as she turned the corner, she was gone in an instant. I had noted the dress she wore; a soft orange colour, decorated with a large dark green and red apple print. It was easy for me to describe every part of what she was wearing.

We have no doubt we saw and spoke to an angel in physical form.
Later, we found out that many people had similar sightings of an angel called the Angel of the Capital Buildings, Sacramento. *Hebrews 13:2 (The Voice translation). Don't forget to extend your hospitality to all—even to strangers—for as you know, some have unknowingly shown kindness to heavenly messengers in this way.*

Other angels minister to believers. *Hebrews 1:14 (NKJV) "Are they not all ministering spirits sent out to render service for the sake of those who will inherit salvation".*

A Seer in partnership with Angels

There has been a massive misunderstanding of what a Seer is. People take so much of what they see literally, but so much of what those who see in the spirit realm is symbolic. For example, a Seer may see scenes of war and conflict but the interpretation of that vision may not mean literal war. It was so at one time but not anymore. We have transitioned into a new age.

Father's Kingdom. We uncover things to bring to the courts in Heaven and then bring the heavenly judgements down to the Earth. Angels love this, when you partner with them, because we show them things to bring into the Father's courts as Sons of Yahweh. The angels don't see what we see. We see it and partner with them in the courts of heaven. When we get scrolls from the courts of heaven, angels are released to bring the scrolls into fruition. This is part of the Angelic's job. They can apprehend things to take them into the court to be judged. This is amazing.

We began to realise I am in a major place of training, like Deborah in the Old Testament book of Judges. The Lord showed us that because I carry the gift of mercy, the angel Zachiel has come alongside me to train and partner with me. Part of this training and judgement will be to judge infirmity, like the man in the Apple store whose arm got healed.

I took my iMAC into the Cardiff Apple store on a busy

Sunday morning for some technical support. I flexed my muscles to carry my computer quite a distance from the car park and then waited at a table to be seen. A young man was super helpful to start with but as the shop filled with people, I sensed he was getting a bit overwhelmed trying to help all of us. Oh yes, I prayed. Abba downloaded words of knowledge and kindness for the young man. Another staff member, who was a large and massively overweight man, appeared then a third person with a damaged arm also came over to our table. One by one I prayed out loud for each staff member, seeing healings and only God knows the rest.

There have been things taking place in my life for purposes of promotion, things I didn't ask for or pray for. Not by works of righteousness, are things which we have done, but according to His mercy.

He said, "I am preparing you to war again." He had these two solid silver gauntlets with Hebrew letters on them and placed one on each wrist. The gauntlets moulded to my body. He said, "I need you for battle," and I didn't argue, I just thought, "This is right!"

Gabriel stood in the distance, a little way ahead. He came towards me and gave me my Sargent Pepper Blue Jacket. I had this encounter previously, years ago, but had not worn my jacket for years. It supernaturally flowed on my body as "General Schroeder." Gabriel has bright blue weeping eyes like Jesus on the cross and he reminded me that I was one of God's Seers and to know that it is out of a place of rest and that He would fight on my behalf. At that time, I agreed but didn't know what it looked like.

When I came home from Germany, I knew that it would be the last trip I would do with COBH. It was a bit like leaving and cleaving because they were like my family. The reality was that when I came to Scotland, I felt isolated, hidden and a loneliness like I had never felt before or even knew existed.

Saint Columba and the Angels

The book *St Columba of Iona* — one of my favourite stories — speaks of some seriously awesome angelic encounters.

On one occasion St Columba addressed the assembled brethren on the island of Iona, making his point with great emphasis, "Today, I shall go to Machair on the west coast of Ireland." He stated, "I wish to go alone and no one is to follow me". But one of the brethren was an artful scout and took a different route, heading south. He took up position on top of a little hill, overlooking Machair, looking to see where the saint had gone. He was curious why Columba had gone alone. From his vantage point, he could see the Saint standing on a small hill. He was praying with his arms spread out towards heaven and his eyes gazing upwards. Suddenly, there was a marvellous apparition — which the spy could see with his physical eyes from his position on the nearby hill.

The witness to this vision should not have happened without the permission of God who desired that the reputation and glory of St Columba should not be made widely known.

Heavenly angels, dressed in white robes, were seen flying down with amazing speed and began to gather around the holy man as he prayed. The angels conversed for a little while with St Columba, then the heavenly crowd left, returning to the heights of heaven; perhaps aware that they were being spied on.

Soon after the angelic conference, St Columba returned to the monastery, where he again called the brethren together. He reproached them severely, asking which one of them was guilty of disobedience. They protested, unsure of what he was implying,
but one man was aware of his inexcusable disobedience. He could not bear to hide his sin any longer. He knelt in prayer, begging forgiveness, in the sight of his brethren. The saint took the brother aside, sternly warning him as he knelt before him. He charged him never to give away the secret concerning the angelic visitation as long as the saint should live.

Due to their reverence for the awesome majesty of God, many saints were aware of the Spirit of the Fear of the Lord. Their intense God-consciousness and the government of God, propelled St Columba, St Patrick and many other Celtic saints to shape the wild islands, changing the face of the United Kingdom forever.

Hebrews 13:2 (NIV) "Do not forget to show hospitality to strangers, for by so doing some have shown hospitality to angels without knowing it." For this is how you are worthy to receive angels while awake. Matt 25:35 For I was hungry and you gave me something to eat, I was thirsty and you gave me something to drink, I was a stranger and you invited me in.

The Unexpected Death of Dad.
I love writing about my dad, especially when the unexpected happens.

At the time I was in London at a conference with Justin Abraham and Ian Clayton, a great conference called *"Tomorrow People."* My dad had problems with his kidneys and was in a care home to allow our family respite time to go on vacation for those two weeks.

I received a call from my sister to inform me that although Dad had managed to have a good night's rest and was coping well, he may have another kidney infection. The care staff had called an ambulance to take him to the hospital. There was no apparent urgency, so I planned to pick him up from the hospital in a couple of days to settle him back home.

Justin decided not to do his last teaching session, feeling he delivered what the Lord had given him to share, so we all returned to our accommodation to take a break. I was tired and soon nodded off to sleep as my friend, Pearl, was lovingly stroking my hair as I lay on the little red futon, my bed for the night.

I woke up abruptly at 4pm. I heard my sister's worried voice telling me that dad had been waiting all day for an ambulance to transport him to a local hospital. He was fully conscious and asked why he was not being fed as he was hungry. Unbeknown to my family, the doctors had not yet picked up on the MRI scan that he had contracted a superbug from his previous hospital visit. He was dying and there was nothing they could do to save his life.

My sister called my son, Samuel and daughter, Ruth. She asked them to come to the hospital to pay their last respects to my dad. They were very close to their grandad who had spent many happy hours with my children at the beach playing cricket, tennis, and rounders and teaching them about the countryside. He liked to pass his skills on to his grandchildren. In the latter part of his life, grandad met weekly with Sam in the village. They played billiards and snooker together in a local Men's Institute.

Later, I was on the phone with my sister who was with dad in the hospital. I remember asking my sister to pass the phone to my dad and hold it to his ear so that I could talk to him. Dad knew it was Kitty, his youngest daughter, the one he'd named at birth when the midwife attended at the sandstone cottage where we lived in Harthill, Broxton. Dad had bought his first brand new black-and-white TV box and at the time of my birth he was watching an advert on the television called, "Kitty Cat keeps a cat a kitten." Oh yes, my nickname after that was called 'cat food'!

My first thought was to pray a resurrection prayer, knowing full-well in my heart that my dad, John Jones, had made the best of things after my mum had died five years earlier. He missed her so much. I didn't cry at first but remember speaking fondly of how wonderful he was, especially when my husband left the family. My dad stepped in to father me and the children during their teenage years.

Numb and amazed, sad, emotional and yet comforted all at the same time. Talking in slow motion to my sister on the other end of the phone, Shalom entered my body supernaturally; the peace that passes understanding.

I instantly went into a panoramic vision, seeing two large angels. Astonished! I had seen these angels a couple of weeks earlier in a vision. They were accompanying my mum. It was heart-warming - she was being her usual bossy self. Her stunning dress was white and shimmering. Golden dust was flowing off her gown as she moved. One of the angels had what looked like white mist coming out of his mouth and was breathing into my dad's mouth, breathing back and forth. A wing of the other angel began to slip underneath my dad's body as he lay in his bed — like a swinging hammock. I then noticed a hand come out from underneath the angel's wing.

Psalm 136:12 (ISV), "With a strong hand and active arm, his love is eternal." I knew in an instant it was the Lord's hand coming out from under the angel's wing, putting His hand on top of my dad's hand. They became one hand joined together then I knew that my dad had been given the life of Heaven.

In my heart, I felt his last breath. The first person I saw after my father's death was Ian Clayton. He just put his arms around me, like Papa God. I was so blessed to have my Welsh family around me as I sat on a garden bench, stunned, in my friend Pearl's garden, with Justin and Rachel Abraham sitting quietly beside me holding me and my family in their hearts. Within those few hours, I knew without a shadow of a doubt that my dad was fine in his heavenly home. There was nothing to worry about as he was safe and secure in the arms of love.

My friend Ruth had recently moved house and was feeling very unsettled. One particular night, Ruth was unusually uneasy as she went to bed. During the night while laying on her left side, she was suddenly awakened. As she opened her eyes, she saw beside her — what she perceived to be an angel — kneeling by the side of the bed, looking straight at her. Ruth was astonished and in awe at the sight of this man she described to be her beautiful angel. He had lovely blue eyes and curly hair, dressed in a white garment. His arms were folded and he was leaning on her bed, very near her face. She felt peaceful, delighted and quietly joyful and yet startled at the sight of her beautiful angel. His awesome presence became apparent to Ruth as she sat up in bed and as the reality of his presence really hit her, in amazement, she began to scream, causing the angel to disappear!

The experience taught her that the Lord had assigned this angelic visitation to help and comfort her in her new home. This encounter changed the way my friend saw the angelic help her in everyday life. I love the way *Isaiah 6:1-2 (NISB)* describes Seraphim as a six-winged creature; the fiery ones. The Seraphim who surround God's throne. They minister to the Lord and serve as agents of purification and holiness. The Hebrew root word Seraph means "burning."

The implication in the Isaiah text is that the Seraphim are in attendance around the throne of God, burning with love. They proclaim God's supreme glory, according to Isaiah's vision. Holy, Holy, Holy unto the Lord. Holy means — set apart, sacred.

Budding Friendship Through Angel Lady — deja vu
One time my friend, Rebecca, had a dream of me before we had ever met. In the dream, she was in The Gate Art Centre in Cardiff, Wales. We must note that Ian Clayton was scheduled to speak 3 months after she had this dream of The Gate Art Centre. The Gate Art Centre is a big old church with tiered, old wooden seats going up.

In her dream, I stood in front of the meeting room talking

26

with Ian Clayton and she began to see an impression of white, wispy colours in front of her like a cloud. She made her way to her seat and once she had sat down, I turned her away from this cloudy pillar and prayed for her very quickly. Rebecca said after the prayer, I walked off. She then turned around to see if this white pillar was still there and discovered the wispy white cloud pillar was still there. It gradually became clearer to her that the wispy white cloud pillar was an angel. The angel spoke to her heart to heart (not audibly) and said, "I am so honoured to finally meet you." Rebecca said it was like time expansion. She did not know how long she was talking to the angel and the angel to her. She had the impression that the angel was very masculine.

At that moment in time, in the vision, Rebecca felt the deepest peace and shalom. She said from then on, her friendship with me, when we did meet, was like a sovereign divine friendship initiated by heaven. You can't make these things up, can you?

About 3 months after her dream, Rebecca physically walked into the scheduled Ian Clayton conference at The Gate Art Centre. I was up the front in the worship time praying and ministering to people and noticed a girl in a bright orange-tomato-red dress walking to the big worship space in the room. She handed me a piece of note paper along with a ten-pound note. We both burst out laughing as we had both seen each other before in the heavenly realms. We got so intoxicated with the presence of Jesus that we lay on the floor.

My side of the story is that previously to this, approximately three years before, I came home from work to find my daughter in tears.

Her granddad was in intensive care in hospital following a major heart attack. I sat comforting my daughter and as I did, completely tranced out. My daughter fell asleep from exhaustion as she had been crying so much. In the spirit, I saw granddad lying in intensive care with tubes all over his body. I saw what looked like a fibre optic cable going between him and the machine, helping him breathe. It was like a bright crystal light that began to go down the fibre optic tube and into his body. When the bright light reached his body, it began to jump-start his heart.

I was consciously aware of praying for his healing. My daughter and I both woke up and instantly by the French doors in the home was a woman with dark brown hair and porcelain white skin. She was very beautiful and was wearing a dark red, satin, Christmas dress. In my heart, I asked who it was because in those days I did not know a lot about the angelic. She said her name was Rebecca. We were so surprised we didn't know if it was actually Rebecca or her angel, but I said to my daughter, "Your granddad will live and not die." Granddad lived for another ten years.

So, going back to the original story when I met Rebecca, she had already seen me in her dream, and I had seen her in a vision. It is hard to know whether it was Rebecca or her angel I met, but when we met in person, I knew her and she knew me.

Angel Illume
I used to have no confidence in my "seeing ability" and a precious friend, Emma Joy, was invited to share her

beautiful relationship with Jesus at one of our regular Spirit School meetings. As she spoke about Union, I noticed a kind of faded light bulb kind of light behind her, as she knelt on the dance studio floor. The more she spoke, the brighter it glowed. Illume Angel. A light bulb moment in time and dimensions, the unseen open to the natural eye.

Northern Lights Encounters
Rebecca's story...

I've been intrigued by the northern lights for years; the mysteriously beautiful moving light show in the dark night sky. A friend said she went to see them, and a very rare spectacle appeared; the lights formed into three crowns! Right before her in the sky! I had to go. I heard someone mention once that the northern lights are the angelic and so I wanted to honour these angelic colour lights in the sky! When I paint, I believe I'm creating a portal or gateway into other places and inviting the essence of that place to engage with me through honour.

I started to paint the northern lights and afterwards I texted Janey to tell her what I was painting as I knew she'd appreciate it ... little did I know; she had seen the northern lights show up in the house where she was staying and she had been encountering them that exact same day!!! Wow! I was in Bristol and she was in Wales. Definitely confirmation and we both saw the lights and engaged with them in our own individual ways, but both very honouring. Little did I know that Lindi Masters had been planning a trip for us to actually go to the northern lights too! Again, confirmation and I can't wait for the mystery to unravel even further actually physically being there!

Angel lady deja vu

Rebecca and I have a lot of deja vu together! The two of us really felt today as we were remembering these events, that after that encounter with the angelic Rebecca learned to engage and see angels more clearly. She said she sees this misty white pillar of cloud often. It is there nearly all the time in the Earth realm. So, she said she learned to stare at it, to speak in tongues out loud or in her heart, and the angels then become more visible.

I knew nothing of the councils of the courts of heaven in those days. The Lord would give me little snap shots of people's lives. I only knew a little about the Spirit realm but even in those days I would know whether it was Jesus or God himself.

I had a quick, sudden clear sight of one of my friends, Lucy, dancing with Jesus and they were stepping in and out of each other in a waltz. Jesus was wearing a tuxedo and Lucy was in a beautiful barbie pink flowing gown. This is not the type of clothes she would normally wear.

Then another friend, Emma, had a big bright light bulb next to her when she spoke of an illumination angel. I wouldn't tell the people I saw these things around because I had no confidence in my 'seeing' ability.

Angel with the letter "R" - 21st December 2018

While in Denham Springs an angel with an 'R' engraved on his hand showed up to Mike who was a leader of the church. As the angel touched our foreheads the letter 'R' appeared. It was the Hebrew letter Resh. I heard supernaturally from

Abba, which was something very significant. Everyone was touched by the angel with the beautiful presence.

[1]Resh, one of the Hebrew letters from the aleph bet (röshe) meaning the head, top, summit, chief, the beginning, the top, to lead. It also looks like a Vav which is its original intent, to bend and see around corners. The beginning was the ancient interpretation of the Resh. The early ancient Semitic/Hebrew of Resh is a head of man. The modern/middle Hebrew Resh looks like the top of a head. The interpretation was the head of man. It is man, Resh, able to see around corners to see Yahweh's original, beginning intent.

Resh also works really well with Holy Spirit to bring to pass this great age of peace and shalom which is so desperately needed in our current generations. When the angel anointed our heads with the Resh it was like the Lord giving us peace of mind, commissioned to be part of verbiage in the courts that legally gives us rights to obtain the mind of Christ. Aaron Smith from the Gates of Zion, Alabama, puts it beautifully,
"Resh makes the sound to look and see what he will say to us."
We see Resh is ahead of time or the OLAM. The original intent is for man to live as a glorious light-being with a higher consciousness, in the image of YAHWEH. Amazing! Lastly, Resh's recognised colour is indigo which according to many commentaries works well with the Spirit of Knowledge.

I had prayed all my life and really struggled with learning and memory retention, but I persevered and my mum

[1]Taken from the book: Friends of Eber, 2nd edition, quote Elizabeth Crawley.

was incredible in helping me, but I thought the Spirit of revelation and knowledge might have left me behind. But now in the latter part of my life, it is all beginning to come together. Something has shifted in the way I think now. I have always loved Holy Spirit and the Lord was showing me His original intent for me. That is nuts! While I was a child, in my bed I would be taken in the Spirit out of my

body but someone came and shut it down and it has taken all this time to open it up. But it is the 'now time' for me and I think we will find many people with the same revelation.

Prime Minister, Teresa May - vote.

I had an encounter while on an internal flight in the US with Theresa May, the UK's Prime Minister at that time. What the Lord showed me happened and the vote went her way. That happened to me before when she got elected. The Lord gave me an absolute download and I preached on the kiss.

Circus Ringmaster — 26th November 2019

The spotlight was on me, the ringmaster with a travelling circus. The MC's coming out with me to present the show were a clown and a seal! We were the opening act! The Lord said, "You are esteemed, heavenly family." I saw it like Tinkerbell from Peter Pan. The Lord said, "You are a general, you are a ringmaster, you are like Tinkerbell under the radar, and like Tinkerbell had prepared the land in advance, Holy Spirit is doing the same with you."

The Lord said I was like a general, having been taken in the Spirit in advance to pray over the land and the regions for revival. But I was already commissioned as a general in special operations and the Lord said we have been building for years, a house of the living stones, quality people and leaders. So, Stevie McKie and I visited Dunadd on the 20th of June 2019. We climbed to the top of the mound of rocks and I instantly saw crusader angels with a white bib and a large red cross on the front. These crusader angels commissioned the kings of the past and were preparing to commission future kings.

I saw a woman, beautifully lying down in a grave from centuries past, all dressed in white, pure white skin, alabaster skin. She was the intercessor for the land for Dunadd. Holy Spirit, Holy Ghost.

"Surf's Up Baby"

It was a spectacular tour of Australia from Melbourne to Victoria, ending up at the quirky, quaint Port Macquarie. Every morning at 5 am and in the evenings, Carol was "Surf's Up Baby".

This is Kate's story: Carol and I were really excited to be part of the meetings and worship in Bairnsdale, Victoria, Australia and especially seeing as to how the Lord opened up a well of healing and salvation there. I then had an expectation that in travelling to the next place (where we had some established relationships in the Spirit), that the worship and the meetings were going to take off!

On arrival at the first meeting, I was surprised to find that there was not the spiritual opening there that we had expected, there was even some hostility in the spirit around the leading of the worship. I was upset but grateful to the Lord who had spoken to me again in Bairnsdale about a lavender field and how important it was for me to turn inwardly into the seat of rest. This proved to be a great shield and blessing.

Another blessing was that in being around my like-minded friends, Carol and Petra, my seer realm was much stronger than I was used to. Later in the week, Jane Schroeder was speaking at a ladies' gathering and while she was up at the front telling stories, I was surprised to see a snakes and ladders checker board clearly appear in front of me, and then it suddenly snapped shut. I felt a heavy weight lift from around my shoulders and the Lord showed me a fat python, a strangling religious spirit was lifted off my shoulders. It was such a relief! I felt like He was releasing me from the 'ministry game' with all its hopes (ladders) and dashed hopes (snakes) and that I was free to leave the game. For days after that, I felt like I had been born again. I was giggling and feeling light and full of joyful RELIEF. The next day when I was in the shower I saw a green angel. She seemed to be associated with the ocean and I asked her what her name was and I felt she said Sho-el, (like ocean shoal). When I asked the Holy Spirit what it meant I felt He said Show — El, (or Show God). This seemed to me to be part of my real mandate; I was to work with the new angel and others to "show" His goodness, beauty, wonder, kindness, love and majesty in the Earth.

I neglected to say that I really felt that the Lord used the breaker anointing that Jane carries to set me free. Your obedience to follow Him and come to Australia and all that He has brought you through carries great weight in the Spirit and it lifted a great weight off of me. Thank you, gorgeous woman. You carry huge influence in the Spirit realm and things shift wherever you walk.

That's my story. Lots of Love, Kate.

Beach Head Walks With My Father
by Jane Schroeder

Amidst folklore tales of dragon's lair.
Small bunny rabbits roam
Wild and free
On grassland beauty deity.

Creation says: "Come
play with me, Let's
slide,
Down the fiery tails of Seraphim."

Who's darts pierce to my very soul,
Heart to kill,
Burning passion
Prevents the drill.

I look up, there on its Beach Head throne, Sits
the Seraphim
With blazing rule,
Mountains melt like wax before it's flame

Lightning flashing all about its deity
Perched on Irvine hill,
Staring out to sea
With its burning will.

The humming birds fly high above,
The eagles soar,
A red kite swoops from hatched babies' nest

All fluffy feathered from mummies breast.
Under the shield of him who knows best, Abba Father.

I hear the sound of distant lands roaring Deep
cries out deep to deep,
Celestial sounds boom far and wide.

Blue cloudy inky skies,
Faces shine forth on crystal seas of glass.
Irvine green fresh river upon the estuary of sound.
A frequency of ecstasy,
Green and pleasant land, Oh, bonny Scotland Oh, brave
you are
Thy beauty shines for all to see

In your ruggedness you rally forth your troops
Where stains of love have strewn the land
It cries for vengeance
Urgency.

Oh, fiery breath!
The piercing heart of rainbow colours
Rainbow seas.
We smell your burning heather roots

The gorse all prickly
Crown of thorns,
Did e'er such love and sorrow meet?
Demands my life my soul my all.

In silence, stillness underground Moles
burrow, interconnecting, feasting
On their wormy captives

36

Eaten alive.
Freedom is our daily bread.
We are not dead.
In Yahweh we live
Our life source,
Complete

Frequency of sound
We breathe again, Alive in
His immense, entwining
benevolence, Awakened.

CHAPTER TWO
Dreams, Visions and Encounters

Dreams, visions and encounters are Yahweh's way of assuring us that He is awesomely aware of every aspect of our lives daily. Every second of the day, and our walk, past, present and future are intricately woven in the tapestry of His plans for us. We don't always have words for what is happening at the present moment and sometimes it takes years for the meaning of things to unfold. We need to trust the Holy Spirit enough, (and test the spirit of things) to rest in, fall back in and enjoy the supernatural experiences as they happen. They more often than not are bringing us healing and motivation for our lives. I have chosen some beautiful moments that express this, His love for us, enjoy mine and some friend's inexplicably exciting walks with the Father, which I encourage you to start exploring and opening up to if you haven't done so already.

Goldfish on the ceiling, Cassock Russian dancers, Greek Acropolis and more

I had the privilege of staying with one of my close friends, Pat, for four months while I was looking for a house in Wales. She lives in a detached house on a hill called Tree Tops. One night as I was lying in my bedroom, I looked up and could see there were huge goldfish swimming around the ceiling. If I remember correctly there were eight of them, opening and closing their mouths. Eventually, I fell asleep.

Another night when I was at Pat's house, I fell asleep and dreamt that two great big eyes were looking at me, and another eye. They would blink. I noticed the eyes were like car wheels with lightning coming out of them. When I woke in the morning there was no ceiling. The Lord said, "Tell them there is open heaven here."

This was before I learnt about cherubim and I would just blurt all of this out to my friends, because I didn't know how to process my visions, sight and encounters into words. I have a lot of dreams where I am not asleep and not awake.

Cassock Russian Dancers
Before I lived in Wales, I used to live in Chester and used to drive to Wales two weekends a month. On one visit I was in a well-known place in Cardiff, Cardiff Bay.

In those days, about nine years ago, they used to call it the Roald Dahl Basin. It is a big massive open space where events are often hosted. It has random pillars throughout the space. You might recognise it as "Dr Who" and different series of things were filmed there. Right opposite the basin is the old, big, red-brick, parliament building. Very beautiful.

In a dream, I saw a Cassock Russian dancer. I noticed he wore black knee-high boots and a big furry black hat. He began to twirl and whirl around the edge of this bay swirling his arms around like Russian dancers do.

A huge fishing net began to descend in the centre of the bay area. It was a rope net, but the rope was like a rope made of supernatural light. As the net touched the ground, I could see people's arms, legs, heads and smiling faces. Boots, hats and coats were all jumbled together. Brown and black they were. I remember thinking it reminded me of when Jesus said to the disciples that they would become fishers of men, not just fishers of physical fish. All these body parts and clothes. It was funny watching them in the dream. They came together to make proper people and that was it; the dream was done!

I began to realise the rest of the previous dream that I had forgotten that the pillars in the bay were actually golden pillars in a temple, a bit like the Acropolis in Athens, Greece. I remembered in Scripture when a cloud had descended and filled the temple. The glory of the Lord descended and filled the place. That was exactly what was happening there. We fell out in the glory. It was no surprise the speaker began to twirl around and around dancing like the Cossack angel I had seen in the dream. We were laying on the floor wrecked in the presence of the Lord. That would often happen back in those days; I would just lay on the floor because I couldn't even walk.

We stood up eventually and the speaker walked over to us and said he wanted us to huddle up together. There were eight of us. He said, "Look up!" and it was cloudy. When he raised his hands, the cloud parted, and the sun came out in the blue sky. We took a photograph as he prayed and on his back was a two-foot-long strip of white light, which was visibly clear in the photograph. He began to tell us about heaven, and said we are going to go into heaven and go higher and higher.

He would say, "Can you feel the heat on your body?"

And, "When you feel cool, you have ascended to another level." He would wait for us to do that. It was my first time knowing that my spirit went into heaven. My body shook and vibrated. I was a little bit shocked and felt scared. I shut my eyes to concentrate and was instantly on a sandy, rocky island. My friend put her arm around me because I was shaking, and they could tell I was afraid. They weren't afraid at all … only me.

One woman said that she experienced that she was in a river by a tree — the tree mentioned in Ezekiel for the healing of the nations. That is when I learned that feeling is seeing. The speaker said, "Don't lose your concentration. If you can't see, just feel your way around." That's in your mind's eye — your imagination — that's how you start bringing your visions/dreams into reality.

I couldn't resist looking into his eyes. They had become a piercing blue colour. That freaked me out. I could see Jesus in his eyes. The speaker said, "Somebody has dropped out!" and I said, "Yes that is me." I'd dropped out because I was scared and the speaker knew me.

Afterwards, the group and I went to Starbucks. I was crying and felt absolute unworthiness because I felt really bad and like I had let the group down. They had stayed in the encounter when I had left. I was annoyed with myself that I didn't complete it, but when I caught up with them later, they were lovely and said it was ok.

When we had prayed for the meeting, I felt the angelic presence around me, and they placed a crown on my head. My friend, Grace, who was with me down at the bay said she saw me clothed in majesty. And one of the guys came and put his hands on either side of my head and just prayed for reassurance into my heart and life.

This next part gets crazy! The meeting started and Justin's wife grabbed one of my hands and Justin the other hand. The rest of the intercessors held hands and we were all in a row. The worship band was playing and the main speaker was chanting and singing a song like, "Dig deeper, in Wales there is gold in Wales."

My whole body began to feel like it was being squeezed and I felt like I was going to take off the ground. I looked over at the speaker and I saw a being step out of his body while he was on the ground. I walked to the back of the meeting place and there was Jesus and the speaker at the back of the room, dancing. The speaker had left his body in the Spirit. I used to think it was hallucinations and I used to have so much fear in those days, it was scary and all too much for me. Now I want more of it!

I don't remember a thing and I just shut my eyes and we just worshipped for hours. I had never experienced anything like this before in my life and all this was very new to me. The atmosphere was super-charged and at the end of the worship set, that seemed to go on for days, I watched the speaker's spirit step back into his
body. He then just stood up and ended the meeting. We were told we can't touch this guy or pray for him. We cleared up the chairs of the meeting and I noticed a circle of people around the speaker.

They grabbed me and had me join the circle. His hand was facing up and we would put our hand into the circle. The presence of the Lord was so strong I fell out in the

Spirit, but someone picked me back up and he touched me on the head and that same white light I had seen outside cut through me. The speaker said to me, "Doesn't that feel good, Jane?" How did he know my name? He didn't even know me!

I couldn't take any more, not even walk to my car so I got my daughter to help me. I could not speak and I was in shock that whole season because I could not comprehend all the heavenly experiences at that time in my life. I used to try to explain things but my friends were as limited as I was in those days. We were just glad when Ian Clayton came along and helped explain things.

I would have encounters while I was at work, or anywhere. I wouldn't pray or ask for these encounters, but they would show up for three years. I would be tranced out. It was like the Lord rewired my brain. Even as we were talking about this encounter, right now — we could feel it. As I read through these encounters in my diary, He pulls at us, because He wants to be close to us all the time. I remember the song: *"Where do you go to my darling when you're alone in your bed?"* I always feel that the Lord is wanting to be 'in' our heads all the time!

In February 2009 in Guilford, London, we did two nights of meetings with Justin Abraham. In the morning we would pray together, Justin would share and then we would walk on the streets. We went there often so I wondered if it tilled the ground for the Ignite HUBS to take off.

I remember one time as soon as we went out on the streets, we saw a white eagle hovering over the area. Two others in our group saw the same. The Lord showed me that Poland is a white eagle and that it means "We are called to the light of His presence." On the Polish flag, it actually stands for, "The light of God's presence."

On the Streets were Monks and Nuns

We experienced His presence when we were on the streets in Wales and it seemed everywhere we went there was a habitation of the light of His presence. Funnily enough, this season I am teaching on the frequency of light as well.

One time I had trouble sleeping, before the Guilford meetings and had a dream. The dream was about an old brown suitcase that was strapped on top of a car in old-fashioned roof racks. All night in the dream I was trying to pull the suitcase off the car and in the end of the dream the Lord opened the suitcase. It was full of the sacraments. In those days my friend Grace and I would dress as nuns, as an honour to the sacrament, on the streets. My daughter bought me bright red rosary beads from the Sacre Coeur in Paris. When we visited there, we went in and the presence of God was so beautiful. I haven't worn them much lately. They are so beautiful and remind me of the presence of God we met at that place in Paris. That day we went on the streets and prayed straight away for a girl who wanted to see through God's eyes. She was a dancer and she was amazed we knew that she was a dancer.

We then went into a Sky TV shop dressed as monks and nuns. We felt a real presence of God as we went into the shop. We found out the man in the shop had a really bad hangover from the night before. He was amazed we were as drunk as he was. He asked us how we got so drunk and we told him we had a Jesus hangover. He laughed and laughed and couldn't understand why he was laughing. We told him it was the presence of Jesus making him laugh.

One time we had three guys that came with us from Barry Island in Wales. Barry Island is famous for a TV programme called *"Gavin and Stacy."* These three had just come back to the Lord. One of them played an African drum and he began to play out on the streets, and two-hundred people gathered. They came to see Jesus. I went and prayed for a policeman on a police bike and he asked what we were doing. I said, "Against such things, there is no law." He agreed and let me pray for him! We invited everyone gathering around the drums to the evening meeting.

That evening gold dust and silver began to pour out onto all people.
   Something very special happened when our friend stood to do the offering. He was never very keen on offerings and was always very short. This night he said there was an angel called Gabriel just blowing a trumpet. It felt like liquid honey oil trickled down our ears just at the moment Justin was talking about provision.

Grace and I were invited up to pray on each side of the offering and to share what God had been doing during the day, but we were hammered drunk in the Spirit. I laid hands on everyone that put money in the offering. A long time after the meetings Justin had emails and messages to say a lot of people received amazing financial blessings and miracles from that evening onwards. That was amazing!

I used to have so much visitation in those days and the

presence of God was on all of us. I remember sitting in bed that weekend and crying out to the Lord for more of Him. After crying out for more of the Lord I looked at the bedroom wall while going off to sleep at my friend's house (I was sharing the double bed with my daughter) and it was like the wall turned into a smoky grey cloud. My daughter and I both saw it. I asked the Lord if it was the cloud of His presence. Then a golden cup which looked like it had real blood in it appeared. He said, "Take a drink" As we put it to our lips it was fine, beautiful red wine. A cup of wine, a cup of suffering. Were we prepared to partake of the blood of suffering, but it became so sweet. Jesus taught me later about a cup of blood, cup of suffering analogy.

Bracelet of light

Not long after that we had a lady called Michelle Parry come to Wales. She had one leg and problems with her stomach. She had spent time with Iris Ministries in Mozambique and I had the privilege of driving her around and hosting her and we would have breakfast together in the mornings. During the night the Lord came to me in a dream and in the Spirit, He clipped a bracelet of light onto my wrist. At the end where the gap was, there were two balls. He said if you twist the balls in the bracelet, an angel will appear. It was in the days when I didn't understand holograms. It was like a hologram angel. The Lord told me I never need to be afraid because I carry the Lord's light on my wrist. I remember telling Michelle of this experience at breakfast. Michelle did not seem surprised and merely agreed with me saying that this was right.

I remember waking up one morning feeling warm pink lips against my lips. I said to the Lord, "This is very intimate!"

and He said, "Yes, the kiss is where we morph into each other, it's in the kiss."

As a child, I had many bad experiences with dentists. I had terrible dreams and developed so many fears. At age sixteen I had a terrible toothache, so the dentist gave me gas to calm me, but the gas didn't work. They thought I was under the gas, but I saw and felt it all. I was terrified and yet again I struggled with why God allowed that. In 2009 I developed a toothache and my daughter came and prayed for me and in the morning, I had no more toothache.

This spiritual bracelet of God's light helped me overcome so many of the fears I had developed as a child. God said he would comfort me from all the terror associated with my teeth. I realised the Holy Spirit was with me all the time.

Yet again I had an infection and a lump in the roof of my mouth the size of a plumb. People prayed for me. It was the worst and I was due to go on a holiday with my two children. Some dear friends of ours had organised an apartment in Spain. We managed some cheap airfares and I had planned to go back to where I used to live and work as a hairdresser in Chester so that I could see old hairdressing clients. This would give us spending money for our trip in Spain, but I didn't know how I would be able to do the hairdressing work as I was in so much pain with my tooth.

As funds were short, I went to a hospital where a student dentist took out the tooth. Unfortunately, the tooth broke. In order to get the rest of the tooth out, the wall of the roof of my mouth was cut and they stitched me up and sent me out. It was a long procedure and by the end of it, I was in such a state. I was in shock! My daughter had to drive the car home, for four hours, on 'L' plates.

She was amazing. I had so many stitches in my mouth and the painkillers didn't even touch the pain.

We got to Chester and stayed overnight with my mum and dad. It was a relief just to be in the family home. My dad was brilliant in comforting me. I worked for two days hairdressing for the expense money for the holiday, working through the pain.

During the 10 days away, my mum unexpectedly died. It was crazy. At 4:30 in the morning, an angel woke me. I saw the angels come and take my mum.

My son was so sick of me complaining about my mouth hurting that he cut the stitches out. The pain was from the stitches being so tight but unfortunately I was left with a hole where you could stick a finger into my sinuses through the roof of my mouth. Because of the hole in the roof of my mouth, I used to dribble a lot. I would pretend it hadn't happened and that I was just blowing my nose.

At that time in Cardiff, I had a specialist who referred me to a young dentist charging half price to put in implants. For six months I had regular appointments while he prepped my mouth to receive a new tooth. Of course, I was terrified, but I used to press my spiritual bracelet for comfort during our appointments.

During that time, I had the privilege of looking on a computer with my dentist, about designing the intricacies of my new tooth. Even at half price, this was an expensive operation but the Company of Burning Hearts offered to pay the fee. Someone I hardly knew put the money for the operation into my bank account.

On the day of the operation, my good friend sent me an album by Kimberly and Alberto Riviera. It is called "The Sunroom."
The dentist put headsets on me and let me listen to this beautiful relaxing album while he operated. This was a major operation where the dentist had to do a lot of cutting yet I felt no pain. The operation was such a success the dentist presented my case at a conference in Portugal. The young dentist passed his exam. At one of my check-up appointments, my dentist told me how his business was prospering and then he referred me to one of his colleagues closer to my new home in Scotland.

Sometimes I wonder why these things have happened and we may never know why but this is what I have received so far. We, the dentist and I, had six months of sharing. He was someone I may never have met outside of a dentist chair and during these six months, I had to go lower with my faith to see other faiths through God's eyes. The dentist asked me to pray for his family, which was amazing and in addition, I felt like God completely healed my bad dental experiences. My tooth is now perfect!

My Friend John
My friend, John, was in his seventies and we found out unexpectedly he had pancreatic cancer. He tried his first lot of chemotherapy and decided that unless God healed him, he was going to go home to be with the Lord. We were all devastated. John was a real father to millions of people including my husband and children. He was given many words about Hezekiah from the Old Testament who was

given extra years following a diagnosis of death.

But that sadly didn't happen for John. They didn't expect him to die so soon but he put himself into bed with worship music and his bible. We would visit and he was still smiling and giving words like a father. He had decided he was done and "nil by mouth" was his choice. He had read about death from pancreatic cancer and decided he did not want to go through this. He went into a beautiful hospice, where they expected him to go to hospice and come home again. He went down quickly but was smiling and loving to his last breath. We learnt that one night my son, Sam, had gone to visit John. Sam was only twenty-one at the time and he had scooped John up in his arms and carried him to where he needed to be carried to. The compassion in my son was so strong.

Within three days of John going into the hospice, I was transported in the night into his room. I stood at his head and there was shimmering, shining Jesus at the foot of his bed. At first, I thought it was Holy Spirit because of the translucent, hazy, bright light that was surrounding Him, but it became clear that it was Jesus and He leaned over, touched John's bare feet and I woke up in bed, back in my room sensing and feeling the presence of Jesus all around me.

On the third night we went to visit John and when we arrived a precious young training nurse told us John was dying. We were called to the hospice and my friend went into the room. She said a light appeared and John took his last breath. I told her what I had experienced the night before. The encounter was a massive comfort to all of us, but we were also devastated.

Turning the Other Cheek

On one occasion five of us went to Lyon, France. We were put up in a crazy hotel with a long passageway and we were right at the end. Nice rooms though! One night, as we were going to bed, we heard a loud knock at the door. We weren't expecting anybody, so my roommate, Bec, went to the door and asked if anybody was there. When Bec didn't see anyone, she got back into bed. Then there was a gravel noise outside the window and we thought, this is not very good. We thought that some "being" was looking in on us. So, I just turned over in bed and said, "Look at my back! I'm not engaging, I am ignoring you!" Things seemed to happen at night.

We had been really tired because we had been up very early, as we had calculated the time change incorrectly. We were ministering many hours in the day and night. I was really annoyed with our host for constantly overworking us for such long hours. When we got to the one meeting, she was rude to me and I asked her what the matter was. At the meeting Holy Spirit told me to honour the woman and she ended up weeping.

We asked the hosts for a little rest and that is when we had an encounter. Rebecca and I went for a rest in the afternoon and as we lay down a cloud appeared above our beds. We had our eyes shut and I was talking to Bec who was in the next bed. We sensed someone dropping down from the cloud. It is not unusual for someone to drop down from a heavenly cloud. It was a man and he spat into both our mouths, something like eucharist wafers. We felt to look up and a big jug was pouring honey into our mouths, more than we could contain. There was so much joy on it. Our visitor was Enoch.

In the same way he walked out of the cloud he ascended into the cloud. I have lots of encounters like that. People just drop out of the clouds. This encounter made us feel really special because I believe Enoch brings infused revelation.

Morrison's superstore, Garston, Liverpool

Angela Gibaud, my beautiful best friend, was coming to the end of a seven-year battle with cancer. I was en route to cheer her up by doing her long curly hair. As I drove past a well-known supermarket chain called Morrison's in Garston, Liverpool, I went into a strong visionary state. Very clearly, I found myself in Angela's large bedroom. As she lay in bed, I saw Jesus standing over her chest.

Radiant white, spinning, twirling motion began to pull Angela's inner Spirit body up into the most stunning captivating waltz.

It seemed like a lifetime as I watched, hovering to one side of her bed. I felt to look up above Jesus's head and saw a kind of funnel of shimmering gold flakes of light. This is the only way to describe what I was seeing.

Angela wore a long, flowing, pure white bridal gown and she waltzed with her lover, Jesus. The gown's train on the back began to appear like gold dust, a little at first then like rain it sped off the dress in all directions. The air and atmosphere were a golden glory cloud. Up, up and away into the heavenly realms, the two lovers twirled in their sacred dance.

Nest conference called Origin

Ian Clayton drew these dots on the whiteboard.

I was going to be staying at Theresa Bowen's. I was a bit shaken up as I had experienced a difficult situation prior to arrival. Then I was moved to a place nearby.

Meet and Greet

Celebrating the smaller things in a private place. I was at the "Meet and Greet" prior to the conference and everyone was enjoying catching up.   I had a thought to look down to the carpet and saw so many small gemstones on the floor. I picked them up and as my friend, Theresa Bowen, prayed with her hand over the small gems they grew in size. A little while later Theresa saw a reflection on the ceiling which was like a small dot of light. We called it the "beamers". The beamers made lattice-type patterns on the ceiling and it reminded me of the scripture, which for me is an "opening up" scripture. *Isaiah 60:8 (New American Standard Bible 1995) "Who are these who fly like a cloud; And like the doves to their lattices? (The Passion Translation) says it like this; 'Who are these who fly like a cloud; And like the doves to their windows, open portals."*

Later in the conference, Ian Clayton drew a similar picture of the dots we had seen. This was such an encouragement to me because it showed me how God can speak to us in what seems to be the smaller things of life and as we celebrate them the "dots" connect and become significant.

God gave Aaron Smith from Gates of Zion, Mobile, Alabama the OPIE which stands for OPEN PORTAL ENTERPRISE. The simple Hebrew letter Yod (the dot, the atom, the awe spark of Ruach Yahweh, in every letter in everything). Aaron began to expand on this, that light-based photonics technology, computers with light, beyond quantum and non-binary.

One Christmas with Kat Kerr

Kat doesn't go to bed; she sits up because she doesn't want to miss an encounter. She usually rests about four hours a night and instantly gets taken up into heaven. I got to sit with her and had to leave and go back to my friend's house because I thought I was going to die. I felt like I was going to be smitten. The presence is so pure around her. She talks to the Lord face to face. I thought that I have intimacy with God but nothing like this. I didn't feel guilty but encouraged to draw closer to God. I didn't need to repent, but I couldn't explain. Very few people I have ever met have I felt like I did, as this way, around her. Heaven just opened up with her. I told her that on the last night and she said it was up to me to keep it open around me.

The Lord was teaching me that the weapon of the Lord is the angelic host, the Lord of Hosts, the Defender of God, the Commander of the angel armies and because we are the sons and daughters of God, we need to command them. The Lord reminded me of a word years ago from Jeff Jansen, "A time will come when angels will come to you and you will give them orders and send them out!" I actually engage them now and no longer just do it by faith. It was a massive divine appointment for me. I now know what to say to them, I see them and engage with them, and I know how to do it now. I slipped into another realm.

More Butterflies

During this time, I had an encounter with a huge butterfly. When I looked closely to see, I saw the appearance of an angel with huge
electric blue wings. I don't know what was going on with the butterfly thing!

There were loads of angels walking through the meeting and I could see them at my friend's house, in the garden. Clearly, the supernatural screen opened up! While I was seeing the angels covering the whole floor in the sanctuary, I saw blue sapphires and diamonds. I perceived we were in the sea of glass. The angels were walking past me in the meeting and the interesting thing was that Kat Kerr and the leader of the church showed up wearing the same blue colour.

Some of the angelic butterflies had turquoise blue wings. I recalled at that moment another time and place where I had first met these angels. A similar electric-blue lightning was once coming out of my belly button and I was able to communicate to God, through cardiognosis (heart-to-heart talk) this way.

The Lord asked me a question - why I hadn't been engaging and talking with Him through my electric-blue belly button but He was clearly speaking to me now. Then Kat Kerr got up and at the end of the message the Lord was telling her to release mantels of the lightnings of heaven. As she prayed for everyone in the room, she slapped her hands together and John G. Lake was standing next to her in the cloud of witnesses. I asked Kat after the meeting if she knew that, and she said, "Yes he is with me!"

While all this was going on and I was supercharged with the angelic, my fingers had gone stiff and blue light was shooting out of my hands. It was so intense that I thought I would explode, so I decided to share and share alike. People got blasted and then they asked me to go to the back of the church hall where two ladies sat. One lady was hooked up to an oxygen machine. I put my hand on her tummy and the Lord said there was an unhealthy mass in her belly, (this was a word of knowledge). The worship was so loud I couldn't communicate to her in words, so I just kept praying for her when my hand slipped into the supernatural realm and into her belly. (As I am remembering this, I am wrecked all over again). It was like slow motion. I knew the mass was cancer. My hand just went 'switch' through the wall of her stomach. At the same time, the other lady sat next to her, and when I laid my hand on her shoulder to pray with her, I became the laparoscopy camera looking into her. The truth was that I was freaking out! I went around her body and around her arteries, looking for sickness and disease. I prayed for her and then I came all the way back again, out through her belly. The pastor stood next to me and I was completely in shock as I told the pastor what happened. I was thanking God, and the pastor said he would get back to me after the two women had a medical report. This should be normal everyday happenings because healing is the children's bread. It was a bit freaky to start with, but I settled into confidence with the Holy Spirit's guidance.

John G. Lake — Lightnings of God

The Lord showed me that John G. Lake walked in miracles from the lightnings of God and when he stood next to Kat Kerr, he was administrating together with her. Kat Kerr kept saying, "You are the host, with the most, who made the enemy toast! Remember this whenever you are afraid."

Gaze
by Jane Schroeder

Your eyes are on me always,
Always
You never break your gaze
You never break your gaze
Above the mighty waters
I gaze upon your face.

Oh, how I love you You
never break your gaze,
You never forsake me
Your melodies of love over me
You over shadow me, always,

Your eyes are on me always
You never break your gaze
You never break your gaze
Your Love is irresistible Jesus,

You over-shadow me always,
In total weakness and surrender
As I behold your face,
Radiant rainbow kaleidoscope
Never changing gaze,
As I look upon your face
I will never break my gaze.

My heart swell in my chest Bursts
forth with in passionate Love
Rejoice in the vulnerability of being a bond-servant of Jesus

CHAPTER THREE
Mission Accomplished

These stories are where I see the manifestation of God (Yahweh) accomplishing things in mine and other people's lives. Through the outworking of the Holy Spirit (Ruach Hakodesh), God always
finishes the work, just as Jesus (Yeshua) came and walked in human form among us on this earth. His sole purpose is to reconcile us through Salvation back into a relationship with God; He said those most famous words, "It is finished!" as He hung on the cross and willingly gave of His life for us. So it is in our lives; these marvellous encounters in the Spirit accomplish and finish things, (maybe even start a journey to the finishing line) with and in us.

In the Philippines 2017
I was sharing a room with a lady who had a raging chest infection and ended up in hospital. There were long days teaching in crazy temperatures. Meditating on *Isaiah 61:1-3* *"To bestow on them a crown of beauty instead of ashes; the oil of joy instead of mourning and a garment of praise instead of a spirit of despair."* One early morning when dawn was appearing through the cracks in the curtains at the windows, Heidi Baker came to my bed, kneeling at the foot of my bed. Bowing down and rocking back and forth as she read, she explained this passage in scripture. (This was stuff I had never understood before this moment in time).

Speaking to me directly, she said, "You have been through many ashes of tears, but the ashes are symbolic of the garlands of love, mercy and great grace." In fact, a couple of days before, Ruth Filler had prophesied, seeing in the heavenly places the number five, meaning that grace, great grace, was in and around my life. Number five in the Hebrew alefbet is the Dalet which means the open door, to see, feel, hear visions, and encounters with God Himself.

I engaged with the woman of ashes. "You have been through ashes of tears, but the ashes are the garlands of love." I wish I had engaged with Heidi Baker, but I was so shocked. It was a mercy thing. The time Heidi Baker came to my bed she was explaining Isaiah 60, beauty for ashes. This was stuff I had never known.

Bali Blog 27th November 2019

I love to share real-life stories, especially ones from one of my favourite places on the planet, Asia. A dear friend and colleague, Daniel Black, and his team travelled to Bali for the first time in November 2018. I was invited to share in the evening meeting at a large church where Daniel Black had shared earlier in the morning meeting about the Shekinah Glory dwelling, and the settling of the divine presence of God, and the meeting just blew up with jubilant joy.

That evening when we arrived at the church the atmosphere was electrically supercharged, still with residue from the morning meeting. I was about to preach afterwards and I had been holding a friend, Doctor Sophie's hand which enabled me to stay standing because I kept sliding down on the floor with the heavy, weighty presence of the Lord. Sophie's homeland is one of the wild islands— Ireland. She had been living in Hong Kong for the past sixteen years.

I could feel Kathryn Kuhlman's presence floating, levitating over towards me. She looked straight into my face and said, "Holy Spirit is within you." Kathryn was known for her intimate relationship with Holy Spirit. It felt weird, because Kathryn Kuhlman seemed to be in me and me in her, plus Holy Spirit with us both — all about becoming one, common union, as one body! Strange to tell, I could understand the Indonesian language for a split second, in a moment in time, even though I can't read or understand it now.

My interpreter was also blasted and overcome by the illuminating presence. I kept saying to him, "This is difficult to explain!" as
he was trying to interpret my message. I read four of my favourite scriptures about joy and the crucified Christ, from Galatians 2:20 *(Distilled Translation Version)*, *"I consider myself having died, and now I'm enjoying my second existence, which is simply Jesus using my body."* The place erupted with deliverance. All the team couldn't help but pray for people because they were on the floor getting delivered from "economic spirits", while healing, weeping, shaking, dancing and laughing for joy erupted in us.

Emotional heart issues such as pain left many people's bodies and joy burst out all over the place as we prayed for hours and hours.

I kept saying, "Jesus is closer than you think, open your eyes and look into His face." It was nuts! The Pastor said she had never seen anything like it before! Daniel gave me loads of responsibility.

Set up under beautiful parasols on Bali beach.
We sent people out to bring people in for Spiritual readings that they call barking, (this means where you speak to people passing by your set-up on the beach). A whole group of lads came to have their mail read, (which is a Spiritual reading, words of knowledge). For instance, two of the lads on the team asked if anyone had a dream and would like an interpretation from Holy Spirit. Usually, Holy Spirit will reveal a picture, a prophecy or meaning, us being a mouth piece for life encouragement or healing for the person.

One such woman was selling scarves on the scorching hot, sandy beach; she received prayer for her swollen hand and the swelling went down instantly. We had prayed for the oily healing balm.
Everywhere we went, every shop, everything we did, we stopped and prayed for people. On my second visit to the leper colony in Jakarta, loads of precious people were set free. From this, I now realise that this part of my life must be written on my life scroll because everywhere my friend, Rui Qui, and I ministered together, people were miraculously delivered, set free and healed.

We hired a cart to carry the food sacks full of beef which we gave away. There were so many testimonies from these contacts with people. I hugged, prayed and loved on a woman who said she had lost her husband a few months previously.

Walking on a little further, around a corner, was another woman with the same story about losing her husband. A third widow called for Daniel Black to go over to her, to tell him her story of how she had lost her husband.

Losing a husband could often result in women losing their homes and livelihood. We sat next to her and hugged her, discovering she was blind. With our lovely interpreter, we asked her to look into the light and she said she could see a bit more light. Daniel ministered to her, loving on her, and she began to see a bit more! As she looked at Daniel she said, "Where your voice is, you look like light! You are hairy like a poppa bear." Then Daniel asked if she could see me. All she could see was Daniel like a bright light. Her eyesight was not completely healed but the miracle was she could see Daniel glowing. Supernaturally she saw Daniel as a glowing light and she couldn't see me at all. We continued to pray and she started to weep. She said she could feel my love and compassion and Daniel explained that was because I could empathise with her loss because my husband had died too. I took her through teaching about the cloud of witnesses and how she could see her husband anytime because she could see her husband in heaven. By the time we left, she was beaming and smiling.

What I loved so much about the Bali mission was everyone with different giftings but functioned together with no misunderstandings. Twenty-nine people but we managed it brilliantly.

Much honour to Justin and Rachael Abraham who taught me loads about ministering on the streets in fun, and a love feast of joy.

Sunday Night Was When It All Kicked Off.
Sunday morning there were one hundred and fifty people attending the meeting. The lovely interpreter was really nervous because he had heard stories about me running

around the meeting while preaching, so I kept it easy and slow. I spoke about "We are in Jesus and Jesus is in us, and we are in each other." I called people up for healing, specifically heart issues. (I had Doctor Sophie from Ireland with me).

My interpreter had a heart murmur so we started to pray for him, and he was going crazy and couldn't breathe, almost like he was being strangled. We were praying outside the building where we had held the morning service and it was boiling hot. His dad was a practising healer in witchcraft, so as we prayed, we went through lots of stuff including generational bloodline ties. We put our hands on his heart and though he had experienced some healing before, his ailment would always come back. Holy Spirit shone His light on the root cause and there was transformational healing to completion. He kept looking at us and smiling, saying, "I have never felt this free!" Grinning and shaking his head, he could not believe that he was healed. It was all to do with generational fear and intimidation. He knew no difference until he met Jesus. God's love draws people into His heart and covers all sin. You know when they are healed by the look on their faces and I couldn't stop looking at him.

After this his home situation got so bad for him, he had to move out and live with friends. This is because of the spiritual battle between darkness and the light of God. He still loves his parents very much, praying for them and visiting them regularly. God loves them with a never-ending love whether they know Abba Father or not.

We got to eat fabulous Balinese food after every meeting.

Street food, restaurants and hotels are all amazing. We ate everything in parcels of rolled leaves with garlic and chilli — to stop you from getting sick.

Best food I have ever tasted in the world. We ministered to Muslims and Hindus. God gave us so much strength and help. All our prayer meetings were in the swimming pool. None of the money for my trip came in beforehand — but by my adventurous heart of trusting, by faith, I used my household budget for the whole of my trip. I went away believing by faith. The whole lot came in by my return home, everything to the last penny, paid off! It was a massive test of faith!

Daniel Black – Sacramento Stories – 18th September 2018

The first time I saw Yeshua face to face was a bit of a surprise. On my first trip to America, I took Stevie with me for six weeks. Daniel Black said, "Come over to us to stand with us." We were in Sacramento and drove all the way to McArthur. His House Fellowship church was a lovely little church in the woods in the middle of nowhere on the way to Redding. We sat in a circle and two guys held my hands and others stood behind us praying, with their hands on our backs. One of my friends, who had always been afraid to go deep into the Throne room in the Kingdom of God, went straight over a hill (as she describes it), into the Throne room. The other lady had a romance with irresistible Jesus. The two guys on either side of me would not let go of my hands because as soon as we started to pray, I was taken back in

time to when the native Indians were taken from that land area. I saw unthinkable things being done to women and children on both sides of the situation. I saw Indians scalping and burning soldiers. I saw atrocities, and leaders of the assault on the Native American Tribes. It was so intense I thought I would not survive the encounter, but both the guys sitting on either side of me would not let go of my hands because they felt what I describe as the "runner" coming on me to escape the horrible intensity of the situation.

And then it seemed to calm down but I was still weeping and the man who was leading us all asked Stevie to stand up and jump up and down. The man said, "The Lord is saying you are becoming a king." This was so unfair. They were having incredible encounters and I was in the pit of hell but I knew it had to do with intercession and what I am called to do. I really honoured what was happening to the others and was happy for them.

Then I saw a woman being murdered. It was during the time of Colonel Custard. While I was watching these atrocities there was a big, tall angel who I knew was an Indian. His arms were folded as if he could not intervene. I knew he was a protector and an Archangel. Months later I knew he was Michael, the Archangel.

The leader asked me to stand up and said, "You are a General" I was wearing a cropped navy-blue jacket with buttons down the side. It was a little army jacket. I stood up and thought I would do a "runner," but a wonderful man said, "I want you to move round and round and back in circles."I desperately wanted to say no, but I just did it. I turned around and on the sixth turn, my Spirit came completely out of my body. It was like there were two of me. There was a cloud-like figure and I looked back at myself and sat back in my chair. Once I started the movement, it was unstoppable. I desperately wanted to say no, but I just kept on doing it. Then I noticed a three-pronged razor sword spinning quickly. It came out of my mouth and I thought it would split my face. Then a two-edged sword came out of my belly. The weird thing was the sword coming out of my belly felt like I was birthing and in travail. The tears began to flow and I felt absolute bliss, heart surgery completed.

After the meeting, we were taken to a beautiful wooden log cabin to stay. I got into my little wooden bed and on the curtains was the pattern of the black night sky with stars. I was exhausted from crying at the meeting so just fell asleep.

I awoke at about 2:30 am. My bed was wet, I was wet...I thought I had wet the bed, but I was sweating so much. I sat up in bed and the room was white light, but the light was switched off. As I looked at this white light, four deer walked across the curtain where the white light was and there stood the Lord, hovering about one foot off the ground, in mid-air. I knew it was the perimeter edge of a field and in my heart, I heard Jesus speak to me and say, "If you have seen Me, you have seen the perfect image of My Father, you have seen the Lord," and He stretched out His left hand.

In my heart I wanted to draw nearer but, in my mind, I was really scared. He drew back and I inched toward Him until I was about five feet away. He was beckoning me to hold His hand but when I got scared and moved back, He too would move back to give me space. I was so shocked that I saw the physical face and body of my Lord and then His lips moved and He spoke to me audibly, not just in my heart. He waved His hands in front of me and said, "Jane, make way." I didn't question, I could only say, "Yes."

At this point I fell asleep or passed out - I think I passed out. The dawn came and I woke up, lying in my soaking wet bed. It was cold and horrible. I managed to peel myself off the sheets, walk over to the curtains and open them. Exactly what I thought was in the Spirit or even a dream or vision, four beautiful deer walked past the window. There was a lovely wooden decking leading out into the forest and the Lord stood there, in broad daylight looking at me!

I was so wrecked! I had to explain as best I could to the owners why everything was so wet. I was really embarrassed!

I dragged myself into the shower to get ready to meet lots of people for breakfast. I was crying all day. They laid me at the back of the car after breakfast. Whether my eyes were open or shut the Lord was there. All day, it was so unexpected that I couldn't speak. I can still feel the awe and wonder as I speak of this. We had to pick up my dear friend Rona and her friend later on but all I wanted to do was to be alone with the Lord, not sitting in a car full of people for seven hours! Later, I had the privilege to sit with Stewie, the local county sheriff, and he shared how he had forged an intimate relationship with the Lord while he drove throughout the county doing his job and he shared some of the accident horrors he had seen with the local farming community.

Wipe the blood off of your Jowls Jane!
One time many moons ago as I was out in the States on a busy tour. It was just at the beginning when I was touring

on my own and getting more of my own personal invites. It had been amazing; I had met a friend in Alabama and been to all sorts of crazy places. I had met the most amazing guy from the Brownsville Revival, and we had a quick fifteen-minute lunch where he told me the funniest stories about how many thousands or millions of toilet rolls you need when hosting a revival, and the costs of repairing toilet doors, washroom taps and stuff like that, practical stuff and he was just really funny. He talked about how religious he had been before the Spirit of the Lord whacked him out. He ended up lying underneath these wooden pews and there was all chewing gum underneath them and the Lord said, "This is what you're like, you're stuck, in dishonour and disrespect for My move and My Spirit." It was so intense in those fifteen minutes, I could hardly stand up, but I got some fantastic photos of him and me together.

That morning we had already been to pre-breakfast with a lovely woman from "Young Living Oils", who had been wanting to meet me for years and she said to me, "Why don't you come with us to the meeting tonight and meet Ian Clayton? He's flying in tonight and flying out again tomorrow." I said, "Oh, it's a long way away and we've already been in the car for weeks." Anyway, we decided to go and I slept in the back seat of the car. It was a beautiful black starry night and I'll never forget it! So, we arrived at her house and I didn't realise that she had parakeets and birds. I met her kids, (my partner at the time?). We all sat around this beautiful table while they were getting ready for the Young Living Conference where Ian was the main speaker and had a wonderful time getting to know each other. Well, Ian said to me, "Make sure when you're travelling you don't stay by yourself. Keep in contact with me and arc in the Spirit. Yahweh looks after the orphans and widows and you're a widow." I didn't think much about it as I'm very independent and have always done my own thing, but something on that day changed for me. Anyway, they were all chatting away and Ian was seated against the wall on this breakfast bench area and they sat me next to Ian. I protested and said, "No, no, no, you haven't seen Ian for ages, you sit together and chat!"

I looked at Ian and he smiled at me and all of a sudden, the whole right-hand side of his face came out at me, this great big, blue, lion's head. Yahweh said to me, "You see, the Ox, Eagle, lion, Man? He's operating in the four faces, Yod, Hey, Vav, Hey!" The lion's reflection looked at me, gave a large yawn and went straight back into Ian's head. I don't think it roared. I quietly mentioned to Ian what I had seen. He went, "Shh, shh!" It was hilarious. I flew home the next day.

Now years before that though, I was sitting in a pub up in Beacon Hills in Wales (when I was living in Wales) and there were quite a few of us getting ready for Ian, who had just flown in to do a conference. For years, every time Ian would come for a conference, I had this demonic thing that would come and it would 'trigger me, trigger me!' I would go into fear (there was so much fear in my life) and when I look back, Ian was so kind to me, really kind to me. He was never in my face. I would just listen to him in the meetings, and I would be glad when he was finished and fly home.

I would lo-ho shout, my body would go crazy and I would really struggle to hold the Glory. That's why Ian said, "Come here, come here. I don't mind you manifesting and I can see you're an evangelist and you definitely move in healing, signs and wonders and stuff. Come and sit next to me." He then said, "Get your right hand up in front of you and clench a fist and when you feel that lo-ho power come on you just draw all of that power into you and when you go to pray for people just release the power, BAM!" I practised it. It was great!

I was doing really well. We had meetings in the morning and Ian was talking about the Tallit and the strings on the edges of the Tallit. I was sitting in the front row and as he was talking about the Tallit, he had it on the top of his head and he flung one of these edges over the top of my head. Well, I slid off my chair and I don't know how many hours it was going on for, but I was birthing and travailing. When I took my makeup off there were popped, bright red, burst blood vessels in my eyes and on my skin. It was painful! It was the pressure of bending over and birthing, the bearing down like really having a baby — I had the pain. I don't know how many times I wet myself. I wasn't the only one that this was happening to. When I was at Manchester Vineyard Church, there was this whole row of women, lying on the floor with their legs up, birthing. We were bringing in the new ages of different times, the different seasons.

Did we understand what we were doing? No! But we knew that it was Yahweh! We would often have visitations from Jesus. We would see Him clearly and He would be walking in and out between us and interrupt us. We didn't ask for this. We would see the angelic and they would walk in and out of our bodies.

We would sit at the table in the breaks during these meeting times and Ian would sit just chatting to us, telling us some crazy stories, which at the time I thought were quite crazy, but now when looking back, were quite tame considering. I would sit wide-eyed, listening and Ian exclaimed, "Jane, wipe the blood off your jowls!" Some of the people we were with were laughing so hard. I asked, "What do you mean, Ian?" His reply was full of wisdom, "The season will come when you won't do that anymore and you will stand behind the Strongman and He will fight on your behalf. The season of war is ending and the season of peace is beginning," which we have been going through now.

Hand Picked
by Jane Schroeder

In childlike innocence,
Before the dawn of time
I was handpicked by God Himself, the creator,
A target of His Love,

Bulls eye!

Grafted into the tapestry of Love.
Divine umbilical cord,
Conductor between heaven and earth.
Pipe song of embryo fullness,

Respiratory joy!

Dipping,
        Diving,
                Swimming,
                        Swirling,

Water flumes of life source.
Gateway of formation imagination,
Mainlined in His strength,
Nourishment of sound.

Life Sustenance!
Life existence, sustained, our daily bread.
Jesus Christ!
Bull's eye.

Respiratory joy!

Life,
        Sustenance,
                Existence,
                        Nourished,

        Quenches my thirst,
        in the dry parched land.

CHAPTER FOUR
Time Capsule

There are certain times in our life when the past seems like the present and the present like the past, all blurring into one long story. I have realised that it is because of the prophetic string in our DNA and the story and plan of our scrolls. We can dream about something, have a vision, get a prophetic word or engage in some spiritual way that takes us back along our scroll into the past to bring healing and comfort, then swings us forward to give us hope and a future, then back into the now and reality, to be able to, confidently, surely and with the power of the Spirit and His fruits within us, deal with difficult situations, making hard times look and sound more like a melodious symphony which we couldn't obtain in and of ourselves, but only IN Him... all with the cloud of witnesses cheering us on!

Dream of Bob Jones and John Paul Jackson

My dad was a counsellor and the chairman for our local parish for ten years. He was so good at his job then got sick of it and said, "You have to vote somebody else up."

Dad loved country life. One year.l they had a commemoration in Waverton village, Chester, where we lived and those who were on the council decided that they would ask for prominent members in the community, who had lived in the village most of their lives, to do a time capsule. Dad was asked to write about his family, adding photographs and different highlights of the life of his family, from when we were children until we got married and left the village. It was fun looking at old photos and memorabilia.

The village was divided into two - Old and New Waverton Village. There was a beautiful massive sandstone cross erected on the boundary between the old and new village and the time capsules were sunk into the ground there.

Not sure why, but about five years later I went to bed thinking about this time capsule in my home village. I had a dream and saw Bob Jones and John Paul Jackson clearly, standing in front of me. They had a huge grey rocket-type-shaped bullet in their hands. I knew it was a time capsule. Firstly, Bob Jones pushed the rocket straight into my stomach, and then John Paul Jackson did the same thing, with broad smiles beaming back at me as this happened. I woke up!

At the time I didn't understand what it meant. It was only in later years, when talking to a friend about dreams and seeing in the spirit Kingdom realms, that I laughingly told him about the dreams. Typically of him he said to me, "Janey, that is a really amazing dream. You received impartation and inheritance." My friend and I felt like the dream meant I was part of the Seer family, seeing things in the spirit. An impartation of two Seers, from them to me. Double portion! I have friends who have dreams like this all the time but for myself, this is not such a common occurrence so I know to really pay attention when something like this comes along. We all have a unique relationship with the Lord.

Expect The Unexpected - Bob Jones!

One evening, dictating another chapter of the book to Cathy in Australia over the phone, my lounge shifted into an encounter. I instantly knew the location was Arkansas, Louisiana, where Bob

Jones lived. There he was, sitting outside at midnight, looking up at the dark starry sky rocking in his rocking chair. Because we have honoured him, I can see him. I truly wasn't expecting this though! He said he had come to visit me again and to expect frequent visitations.

Bob Jones indicated it was very key that I went to the Hebrides with my good friend, Stevie McKie, that week. I had just been asking the Lord whether or not this trip was my assignment. I used to follow the crowd because everybody else did.

Bob Jones was actually talking to me. He's one of the 'Cloud of Witnesses'. In different Bible versions it says in *Hebrews 12:1 "A large crowd of witnesses is all around" (CEV) Encircling us (VOL) On every side (TCNT) Since we are surrounded by such a great cloud of witnesses (NIV) Surrounded by all (VOICE).*

The Lord plugs me in - I can't plug myself in - I am an unusual Seer. Bob showed me a lake and the moon was shining down on the lake. Bob had his arms stretched out wide and he was wearing old, blue denim dungarees.

He said, "You have been here many times before to this little wooden shack by the lake and have been too scared to go inside. It is not going to be a scary place, where you have seen loss before, but a place of visitation with the Lord. Even though sometimes it has felt like a lonely and isolated place since you moved to Ayrshire, Scotland, the Lord has you there for visitations."

I have always known in my 'knower' that I would walk on water at night time with the moon shining and shimmering down on the water. Bob said, "I will teach you to walk on the water on the lake." It felt super weird! I am here in my house, but with Bob Jones at the same time, dimensional shift, multi-location!

Bob was repeatedly stretching out his right hand over the water with his other hand tucked in his pocket. He brought out a golden coin which looked old and quite bent and misshaped. As I looked closer, I could see it was an old gold sovereign. "You have forgotten the Lord has given you authority over wind, weather, tides and seasons, Jane," Bob said. "Remember the prophecies of old, the people who have imparted and given into your life, Jane." Memories began to flood back into my heart, the former things that happened to me as a youngster many years ago reminding me of different landmarks in my life to bring me to the present day.

The sovereign represents the sovereignty of God I carry as I remember that I am an emissary to the throne. I can actually hear Bob's voice even now. Freaky! "Do you remember when your husband Rob left you alone with the children?" Bob asked me this question and said, "It was a really hard time emotionally, physically and draining.

One summer's morning you got up and you cried so much that you went to visit your dearest friends Rona and John Scot at their home. You sat on her couch in her lounge when suddenly her lounge became a rowing boat on a lake and you were snuggled up in the front of the boat, in the bow and hull, even though the sea was stormy."

Rona began to speak words of comfort, "When you are in the middle of a storm, the eye of the storm is the safest place." I was in the middle of a divorce and what was going on with the kids and having to take three jobs and the crazy amount of pressure and stress.

Another piece of the vision appeared as Bob stretched out his right hand. Jesus came to visit me on the water as I was about to get out of the boat and Jesus said, "Don't get out of the boat. Stay in the boat, I am coming to you!" Opening my eyes, I could see in the visionary state and Rona could also see the same scene at the same time. "Stay in the eye of the storm, you are going to sit this storm out."

The wake-up call, reminding me of my deep friendship and love for Rona, her encouraging me to not get distracted by circumstances around me and my kids right then.

In the vision the "Ever Living Indian" showed up. He knows Bob and talks to Bob and they were looking at me and laughing. He was rubbing his foot on the ground in the dirt. I said, "Here we go again, he is about to draw me more symbols on the ground that I never understand." I always see the "Ever Living Indian" in the night hours, never in daylight.

"Fire Stone" I call him! As he drew a bridge I've seen before, with a cross at the foot of the bridge he said, "It is time to cross over Jane." I said, "Cross over where?" He said, "You know where you are going." He was talking to Bob Jones again, laughing with a big broad grin, a lovely fatherly smile of affirmation.

Joshua 3:5 & 11-1 (NASV)

Joshua 3:5 Joshua told the people, do all the rituals and purifications and prepare yourselves because tomorrow the Eternal will show you wonders.

Joshua 3:11-17 The Covenant Chest of the Lord of all the earth will pass in front of you into the Jordan River. 12 Now select twelve men, one from each tribe of Israel. 13 When the priests who bear the covenant chest of the Eternal, who is Lord over all the earth, step into the river, then you will see the waters of the Jordan stop as if behind a wall.

14 So the people set out from their tents to cross the Jordan, with the priests carrying the Covenant Chest before them. 15 During harvest time the Jordan is swollen, running over its banks; but when the priests stepped into the river's edge, 16-17 the waters stopped, piling upstream at the city of Adam, near Zarethan, while the water flowing downstream toward the sea of the Arabah, the Dead Sea, ran out.

Then the Israelites crossed the Jordan opposite the city of Jericho, walking on dry land just as Moses had led their ancestors from Egypt. While the Israelites crossed on the dry riverbed, the priests who carried the covenant chest stood firmly in the middle of the Jordan until the last Israelite had crossed over.

At one time Kat Kerr told me that Joan of Arc is always around me because I am a general in the Lord's army. I never understood this but did what the Lord wanted me to do - and I prayed.

Bob Jones was talking to me on the right side of Fire Stone, my ancient native Indian friend, who was listening. "You have come to this point of crossing over many times and you want to do it with your heart but don't know how. All you need to do is one step at a time, don't overthink it."

A rod appeared in Bob's right hand as he spoke. "Jane, you got your rod three years ago in Scotland and have only used it a few times, in destruction. You need to pick up your rod again and not just use it for healing, but to lead and to move things around. The shadow of past destruction is gone." As he handed me his rod to try, he exclaimed, "Try mine," and threw it at me! "This is a weapon of love, not war, Jane, get your head on it!" Holding on to the rod he said, "Let's go somewhere!"

My own rod is the same as Bob's but mine is activated when a huge sapphire stone appears to come out of my chest at speed, landing securely, a perfect fit on the top of the rod, to activate an electric blue, turquoise, lightning strike.

I first received my rod three years ago when I thought it was a broomstick hovering above my head, and I felt the Lord say, "Grab it!" As I held onto it, it literally dragged me around the sky, lifting me higher, higher, higher and higher into a weird planetary system where skeleton-looking beings with elongated heads with crowns on were residing, ruling and reigning. My instinct was to strike the planet. I waved the rod in mid-air, pointing it straight at the beings. Bob's rod works that same way. He said, "Grab on to my rod," and he was already off the ground. I wasn't sure, so he said, "Come on, you want to know what a shooting star feels like, grab the rod!" We went higher and higher. Bob was trying to talk to me the whole time of our ascent, while I was amazed at where we were in the black starry sky. "Don't be afraid of the dark, you have overcome a lot of childhood fear about darkness!" exclaimed Bob.

Every time his right arm stretched out in front of him another part of my past showed up. I was seeing my mum dancing with Jesus as she ascended into Heaven. My mother always looks so beautiful, an iridescent shining pure white light.

I said to Bob, "I can tell in my heart we are going to leave this place," as we began our descent back down through the atmosphere to land beside the cabin on the lake. In the twinkling of an eye, we were sitting on the edge of the deck that leads into the lake, talking and dangling our feet in the water. The lake was like glass and there was a perfect reflection of the moon on the lake.

I have had the cabin by the lake encounter so many times before and didn't know where I was on the earth. I have had the revelation for many years about the waters above and the waters below mentioned in *Genesis 1:1(TPT) 'When God created the heavens and the earth, the earth was completely formless and empty, with nothing but darkness draped over the deep. God's Spirit hovered over the face of the waters.'*

Bob Jones said, "I will have more revelation on this." I asked him to teach me about it and he became a mentor to me. He confirmed he had come to help me reveal, understand and step into where we were going in the next season, to show us more about the ancient path. I thought it would be a Celtic saint or revivalist of old from my nation of heritage who would be sent to teach and mentor me in the ways of the Kingdom realms in heaven. Bob said, "The Lord chooses whom He chooses," smiling a big smile and laughing.

Only that week Ruthie Williams and I had been studying the who, what, where and when of "The Angel of the

Lord" appearances in Scripture. I believe it's the attribute of God's presence, the show-bread, the Hebrew letter Shin's character, (along with all the other Living Letters) I expand more about the letter Shin in Chapter 12.   A bit like when God sent a messenger, John the Baptist, before Jesus, sending part of the Father, His Son Yeshua.

I obviously didn't need to prepare that night for the book dictation. Stevie said quite a lot of "Dove Company" have had visitations from Bob Jones over the years, but I didn't know that… I was shocked and amazed all at the same time!!!

Agnes My Mum - Visitations

Every 29th December, on my daughter's birthday, mum graces us with her presence. A grey cloud appears above my head and simply, mum drops down in front of me.

I didn't have any visitation on my daughter's birthday this year! We wonder if maybe it didn't happen because we weren't in our own homes. It was ok, I knew a visitation would happen. I always expect it and sure is sure, mum graces us with her presence, showing me her new golden slippers, her broad smile, laughing and talking to me. "Look, I dance with your dad in the chandelier room, in the ballroom above the heaven of heavens." Personally, I have been there many times. One day the Lord showed me that the chandeliers are the tears we have cried and have become iridescent, prism effect crystals reflecting light, a dazzling display, a spectrum of rainbow-coloured chandeliers. Jesus walks through and touches them with absolute love, compassion and adoration for the prayers of the saints and the tears they have shed.

Remembering Albion: Story by Teresa Bowen

We had journeyed far into the heart of an ancient land. It was a place of great nobility and martyrdom, where the voices of the past spoke to us from beyond the veil of this world.

As we listened, they told us of a different realm — one from which they had all come. A realm born from the morning itself, birthed upon the shores of Albion. This land was inhabited by those driven out by their enemies - sons of the earth who took to these wild islands, a people of land, sky and sea. The people of Albion lived in harmony as an example of Father's garden. Greed from the fallen, jealous of Father's love, the darkness swept in to remove what was. The stories of the brave never wavering in their faith live on to this day. They are the courage makers in the weakest of hearts - this fiery courage has always found its home in living epistles when all hope seems lost.

The garden paths were long forgotten, overgrown with weeds and brambles until one day, a people cried out and began to clear the way. They worked tirelessly, establishing a garden where beauty and holiness thrived. They invoked Truth, Life and Way. He came to them in Grand Display. The cloud of witnesses told stories of old to those who were eager to hear. The path builders created new pathways so that others could come and worship the Divine as sons and daughters of the Living God. They set high the lights so that light could run and all might see the glory of God shining in this place.

Cool breezes swept through the trees, sunlight kissed the flowers and children's laughter filled the air. The procession of delight continued as realms opened up revealing the secrets of long ago. Before them, they followed the ancient paths to discover hidden wells. The waters of remembrance called to them, inviting them to drink from its refreshing depths. They knew that they would never thirst again.

Poem
by M. M. van Rensburg

Let me be a blue light
To rest your white flame on
I will fold up my old mind
And step into the unknown

Lead by you My loving guide

I have waded this far in your blood
There is no return no falling back
Into rough waters tossed here, there
And everywhere

I make my way towards pure light
Taking gulps from your life-giving
Air

I sprinkle the salt of your Wisdom
on my wick and burn

CHAPTER FIVE

Israel

2019

I sat in peace and tranquillity in the garden near the place called the skull. Yeshua, sacrificial lamb, drawing nearer than a brother. I sensed Him cupping my hand and waiting. A living white dove appeared in my hands in a visual state looking at me. The Holy Spirit would be more of a tangible person from then on. Take off your shoes and socks, pour water over your toes, this is Holy Ground.

My personal experiences in Israel and Poland have given me a deep love for the Jewish people and Israel as a nation. Israel and her people get into your heart immediately, because we are grafted into the history of those people by virtue of the cross and the price Yeshua paid for us to be reconciled to the Father. I cannot fathom the cost of the pain, suffering and blood, but feel the absolute love from the Trinity. Rick has captured this in detail in his sculptures and it has affected me, just as it does so many people who see it daily... A living memory in sculpted form of two worlds meeting as one in memory of pain.

Fountain Of Tears
https://castingseeds.com/ and *https://fountainoftears.org/*
Rick Wienecke, Canadian born Sculpture Artist, as a young man knew if he didn't step out of his lifestyle he would end up in prison. He went out into a field and prayed his first

prayer, "Is there anybody out there? Please help me step out of the life I am living!" The Lord answered his prayer! He started reading a book about Jewish people and the Holocaust, how out of the ashes the reestablishment of the Nation began. As he was reading about their survival, he came to the conclusion that if there was anybody out there, he must go to Israel in search of God. He was convinced that He had something to do with them (the Israelis) and with this land (Israel). Rick, not being Jewish or knowing anything about the Israelis, other than what he had read, was stirred in his heart and decided to go to Israel for six months to live on a Kibbutz.

Two very dramatic things happened to him when he arrived in Israel. Remarkably, the Jewish Government gave him Residency, and instead of six months on a Kibbutz his stay lasted seven years. It was simply a miracle, the Lord proving to Rick that His communication about staying in the land was true. His search for God came to an end and he gave his life to Yeshua.

Rick found it was very difficult talking to Israelis about the love of God because of their History, so God gave him a new creative language, a gift of communicating the love of God through
his Artwork and Sculpture. He began to realise he had a new communication that touched his heart, overriding everything else that was going on, that touched the very core of people's hearts to deep places.

From 1980 -1990 Rick became an accomplished artist. For many years he never felt to work on any pieces of art about the Holocaust.

In 2001 he was at a conference called Pay Back where he was displaying his artwork. The conference had nothing to do with the Jewish people. One night in worship, Rick's life was turned upside down. He had an encounter with God's presence. While weeping he heard God's voice say, "Pay back to the Jewish people!" God was asking him to create a memorial for six million people!

He began a journey of questions and answers with God. What is a memorial to the six million people within Art!

Fountain of Tears' Sculpture – My God by Rick Weinecke, photo by Yohai Wienecke

Stones of Memorial
Joshua 4:4-11 (NASV)
Joshua chose 12 men with 12 stones from each of the 12 tribes. Placing the stones in the middle of the riverbed as a memorial v7.

4 Summoning the twelve men he had selected from among the Israelites, one from each tribe, 5 Joshua said to them: "Go to the Jordan river bed in front of the ark of the Lord, your God; lift to your shoulders one stone apiece, so that they will equal in number the tribes of the Israelites. 6 In the future, these are to be a sign among you. When your children ask you, [a] 'What do these stones mean to you?' 7 you shall answer them, 'The waters of the Jordan ceased to flow before the ark of the covenant of the Lord when it crossed the Jordan.' Thus, these stones are to serve as a perpetual memorial to the Israelites." 8 The twelve Israelites did as Joshua had commanded: they took up twelve stones from the Jordan riverbed as the Lord had said to Joshua, one for each of the tribes of the Israelites. They carried them along to the campsite, and there they placed them. 9 Joshua set up the twelve stones that had been in the Jordan riverbed on the spot where the priests stood who were carrying the ark of the covenant. They are there to this day.

10 [b]The priests carrying the ark stood in the Jordan riverbed until everything had been done that the Lord had commanded Joshua to tell the people, just as Moses had commanded Joshua. The people crossed over quickly, 11 and when all the people had finished crossing, then the ark of the Lord and the priests crossed in front of the people

Ebenezer - Stones of HELP
1 Samuel 7:2-10 (NASV) 2-4
(Narrative of the above scriptures). Israel experienced Revival under the leadership of Samuel. The nation repented of their sin, destroying their idols. Samuel gathered the people at Mizpah where they confessed their sin and Samuel offered a sacrifice on their behalf v5-9. During this time of repentance and renewal the Philistines drew near to engage Israel in battle v10. The Israelites went

out to do battle against the invaders and God sent them Supernatural HELP! On that day THE LORD Thundered with a Loud Thunder against the Philistines throwing them into such a panic that they were routed before the Israelites, a decisive victory! Also, several cities the Philistines had previously captured were restored. Samuel took a stone to Commemorate the Divine Victory setting it up between Mizpah and Shen naming it EBENEZER.

Complimentary reading: *Zechariah 3:8-10*

My own story of 'Stones of Help'

The first time I met Grant and Samantha in New Zealand they prophesied stones of help, 'Ebenezer,' not realising at the time that the Lord would speak to me in Stevie McKie's kitchen. Stevie's words were, "In two years you will move to Scotland to help them build." At the time, my daughter was living with me in South Wales with no thought of her moving back to Chester, or me to Scotland. Two years, almost to the day, Ruthie and Jay were married and moved back up North, literally a couple of days before one of the NEST conferences. This was in the year that I moved out of my home in South Wales to Scotland becoming Janie Pops Mc Schroeder, lol!

The FOUR KINGS prayed for me moving into *Fiery Crown and Glory ministries*, out of the Valley of Dry Bones.

Result

Continuing Rick's Story

'The Fountain of Tears' Sculpture by Rick Weinecke, photo by Yohai Weinecke

Jesus, agonising in the Garden. *Luke 24:44 (NIV) 'He said to them, "This is what I told you while I was still with you: Everything must be fulfilled that is written about me in the Law of Moses, the Prophets and the Psalms."'*

Six pillars of "Burnt Stone" are made out of the stone in the Judean wilderness. (Resembling many who were burnt to ashes!)
Seven panels of the crucifixion Sculptures. (The seven different things Yeshua spoke while on the cross.)
Water trickles down the pillars of Stone like Tears, hence the name "Fountain of Tears." The water running over the pillars represents Jeremiah's tears. The water is channelled out to irrigate six Olive trees behind the wall. The "Fountain of Tears" in Arad, the stones of the crucifixion panels are the colour of Jerusalem stone, (an off-white with light yellow-gold). This represents the colour of the land of Israel. Rick's stunning Sculptures are held in a large tent in Arad in the south of Israel! The panels in Birkenau are grey representing the ash from the camp when it was fully operational and is in a building.

In *Jeremiah 9*, Jeremiah was standing in Jerusalem. Everywhere he looked, he saw death. He cried out to God, "Oh that my head was a spring of water and my eyes a fountain of tears, that I might weep day and night for the slain." Context … Jeremiah was asking God for his words to be heard again for the six million Jews. The Lord hears the cries of our prayers and He has not finished yet! A memorial is a cry through us.

Rick's work has profound meaning if you look at the figures. It's a dialogue of suffering.

2 People
7 Panels of the crucifixion,
7 different things = Jesus' statements while suffering.

The Bronze Figure with a Shaved Head wearing clothing with Stripes on. The Holocaust Survivor, a victim. We need to appreciate the pain and suffering they would carry for the rest of their life, FOREVER! This still remains an open wound for the Jewish people.

The first panel on the Sculptures portrays the Holocaust survivor as hearing the words Yeshua is speaking, trying to understand amidst his own suffering.
Yeshua said, "I am the source of living water, if anyone comes to me and drinks he will never thirst again."
Yeshua on the cross is saying He is thirsty; He is all poured out. The Holocaust survivor understands, "I am thirsty." Tens of thousands of Jewish people died of thirst. You see one hand getting very close to touching the leg of Yeshua; He understands thirst because the survivor's other hand is cupped for LIVING WATER and God is going to pour it on the land.

(Scriptures in the NKJV)
   1. Father forgive them, for they know not what they are doing. *Luke 23:34*
   2. Today you will be with me in paradise *Luke 23:43*
   3. Woman, behold they Son! Son, behold thy mother! *John 19:26-27*
   4. My God my God, why have you forsaken me? *Matthew 27:46*
   5. I thirst…*John 19:28*
   6. It is finished…*John 19:30*

7. Father, into your hands I commend my spirit. *Luke 23:46*
(Read the CRUCIFIXION account Luke chapter 23)

Father, into your hands I commend my spirit.

People asked Rick, "Did you have an intense dialogue with the holocaust survivors?" He replied that he received his inspiration from the Lord, Yahweh, the creator of the "Fountain of Tears." In some cases, he didn't know what he was doing or what he meant, but over time, when Holocaust survivors visited the "Fountain of Tears" memorial, they told Rick what it meant to them. He is still learning more from the survivors even today.

Rick really struggled with this project until he realised and came to understand that what the Lord really wanted was to bring the connected similarities of the suffering from Christ's Crucifixion and the Holocaust survivors together in a powerful work of Art. He thought he would lose everything if he portrayed this, but knew if he walked away from the project, he would be walking away from HIS RELATIONSHIP WITH GOD. What came after were these amazing Sculptures, "THE FOUNTAIN OF TEARS." It was always on the Lord's heart to be seen somewhere else. It's a Miracle, that about seven to eight years ago, it was possible to buy a piece of land in Poland for a building with much more space than the land that was owned in Israel. Rick recreated the "Fountain of Tears" three hundred metres from the gates of Birkenau in Auschwitz, Poland, one of the most horrendous Concentration Camps in the world.

The Lord is Reaching out to Comfort His People. When Jewish people visit "The Fountain of Tears" knowing nothing about Yeshua, it's a Revelation of, "My God My God, WHY Have You Forsaken me!" Interestingly, recorded in the gas Chamber was heard the same thing, "My God, My God, Why Have You Forsaken me?" Often Jewish Visitors come to understand Yeshua's suffering by coming together because of Yeshua's suffering.

Final Piece
Yeshua will take a place that speaks of death and bring it into life! Rick continued to live and sculpt in Israel for over forty years. He is married and has two sons.

Taken
In 2013, in a visionary state, I was taken to Auschwitz. In the vision, an old Jewish man in his eighties was wearing a long, winter, wool coat, hat and red scarf. Slowly taking off his hat, then coat and scarf in a bitterly cold night, he looked up at the dark night sky with twinkling bright stars, and he was seeing his last frosty breaths on the earth as he stepped down a brick stairway into a gas chamber.

A few years later I was back at the same place in a visionary state. My heart had been stirred by an invitation into the courts of heaven to judge persecution and torture. As I stood at a distance this time from the entrance to the same gas chamber, I breathed a deep breath and it was as if I was drowning or suffocating. It was with a sigh of relief that I could breathe and felt life again. Then I saw the same man step up out of the gas chamber, firstly put on his hat, then scarf and coat and nothing could have prepared me for what happened next. As the man walked across the ground of the Concentration Camp again, thousands upon thousands of people followed up out of the gas chambers, smoke vanished, and chimneys were still. The heavenly justice system, the courts that we can officiate in, through repentance, often down our generational lines, can change our future dramatically.

Blood coming out of the WALL!

Painting, decorating and being creative help me relax and one evening, after a long day painting, I was finishing off the chimney breast where a handmade wooden cross hung that my son, Samuel, made to slide photographs into five pockets. I noticed two red spots on the wall where I had just painted. At first, I wondered if I had cut my hand…no! I was using a new paintbrush and roller that I had never used before. I licked my finger, as you do, and rubbed the spots. It tasted like blood! By now, to my astonishment, the wall was starting to bleed. I had recently been reading a birthday gift book *THE LIFE OF ST GEMMA GALGANI*, an Italian Laywoman born in 1878. She lived in obscurity, dying at age twenty-five. Fondly known the world over as "The Gem of Christ" with extraordinary ecstasies and mystical gifts she would sweat blood upon hearing our Lord blasphemed. I wonder if this took place in my prayer of contemplation while thinking about Gemma and my heart's desire for my beloved Jesus.

A Cup of Joy a Cup of Suffering
by Jane Schroeder

Mesmerising twisted body, blood saturated matted hair.

Love and valour flowed, mingled down.
Agonising ripped flesh, fresh jagged wounds palms.
His furrowed brow pierced with a thorny crown.

Crimson tide of sticky liquid love.
Nailed feet of burnished bronze, gouged,
Dripping flesh wounds from saturated white linen hem
Father saw Him scourged.

Swooning in Messiah's presence
I faint at the sight of such glory,
Clothed in His death and resurrection.

'The Fountain of Tears' Sculpture by Rick Weinecke, photo by Yohai Weinecke.

CHAPTER SIX

Africa

Travelling to other countries releases a boldness to speak, do and open oneself up to the Holy Spirit even more. Just venture to a place where no one knows you, in the safety of a team who loves you, and watch yourself grow in very many areas. I thank God for the mighty men and women of God that I have had the honour of travelling with, ministering with and doing life with. I hope you find encouragement to step outside of your box and serve and walk with mighty men and women of valour. Give it a try if the opportunity opens up for you. Serving us is what Jesus did to His fullest.

Kenya 2005 - My very first visit to Africa.
We got on the flight. A lovely African lady sat next to me on my left hand side. As we chatted, she kept getting up and down to go to the toilet. While we were chatting, I felt like asking if there was anything she wanted me to pray with her for. She had a bad back, so I prayed for her. She stood up, went to the restroom and her back was healed. She asked me what I believed in. I told her and shared Scripture with her from my little Bible. It was absolutely a divine appointment and really easy. In my heart, I knew the whole trip was going to be sweet and full of miracles, signs and wonders.

Jack.
We had only met Jack in Cardiff so we didn't know him

very well. We didn't even know if there were arrangements for us to meet him at the airport. We had already decided in our minds that if Jack wasn't available, we would book a hotel and do street missions in Nairobi.

We arrived and we were thrilled to see Jack waiting for us. We met his beautiful wife and he took us straight to his school, called Book Shine. It was a little concrete building in a shanty town. We shared with the class about Jesus. Since then, the school has become a massive, really well-known school with the assistance of better funding. I had the privilege of raising money to provide assistance for the cost of the teenagers' diploma courses and for teachers' wages.

We took flights over Lake Victoria, and my flight was different from everyone else's. We went to Kisumu. Amazingly, my son Sam went there for teaching practice for six weeks, years later.

We had the privilege of drawing water from a deep well and had a go at putting the water pots on our heads to carry the water. I couldn't do it at all. The young women walked miles just to carry water. At the meeting I loved interacting with all the babies, the young mums and the people and I so loved learning about their culture and praying for them.

We were having dinner in the afternoon before the church service at one place and received a phone call to say a young girl riding her moped had been involved in an accident and had split her leg wide open and was in hospital in Kasumi. We felt that two of us should go and pray for her in the hospital. I volunteered to go with a young man from the area. We took a taxi on an hour-long journey into the main great big city. It seemed like hours on dusty roads in this taxi, arriving at the hospital at dusk and at a busy time when there were what seemed like millions of men. The driver and the interpreter got out of the car, locked us in the car and walked away. The other guy and I just sat there with people looking at us. I was about to roll down the window and climb out through the car window and ask what was going on when they came back and said that they wanted to double the money we had agreed upon for the ride. We negotiated and struck a deal and off we went.

It was a very sparse, very poor hospital. We spoke to the nurses and some of them had been working two days without a break. We found the young girl lying in bed with about eight beds around her. Her leg had split from her knee to her foot and it was elevated up on a metal frame and there was blood everywhere. The bandage was soaked in blood, so we began to pray. Neither of us felt afraid. We had complete blind faith that she would be healed. In beds around us, there were children crying in pain as well as distraught teenagers.

We had already pre-agreed on the amount we were able to give towards the young girl's treatment and there wasn't enough money for an operation. The X-ray showed where the bone was completely shattered and snapped off, with one bone behind another, which would require an operation. The young girl was so scared and shaking and during this waiting time we got to meet her mum and dad. We prayed for ages and the young girl started to feel pain relief and her leg stopped bleeding. We prayed for many children on the ward and then we left.

We got back in the taxi with the driver and were halfway home and realised they were taking us on a much longer way home and asked us for three times more money than we had agreed. We were in the middle of nowhere, so we couldn't get out and walk and were completely at their mercy. The team back at the hotel were praying all the time and beginning to worry as it was very late at night and we should have been back already. It took us three hours to get there and five hours to get back. When we got back to the hotel, we gave the taxi driver the amount God told us to give and walked off. We had to have a lot of faith, be confrontational, bold and gracious while relying on the Holy Spirit. Kenya is where I first started to really see in the Spirit.

Two days after the incident of the ride to the hospital, we were in the middle of nowhere at a church. There were lovely people in the middle of a sugar cane field. We got the phone call about the girl being healed to say they had taken an X-ray before the operation and the bone had knitted back together! The money we gave them paid for all the medical and hospital bills. We were overwhelmed and praising God.

We went one day up a local community's sacred mountain. At the bottom was a woman dressed in bright colours of red, yellow, blue, starving herself to death. One of the men in our team boldly went over to her and prayed for her. We had no idea of the outcome; all was done in faith. We prayed for a distraught girl from another tribe who was married, but her husband went off with someone else and she wept in his arms. There were so many encounters like this, and it reminded me what I am really supposed to be doing.

Faith

Hebrews 11:1 (TPT) Now faith brings our hopes into reality and becomes the foundation needed to acquire the things we long for. It is all the evidence required to prove what is still unseen.

Kenya was a significant time for me because it brought value to my life and it made me confirm that I have been called to nations to pray for people and the Lord used me to see healings. While in Kenya, I had the impression to wear lots of T-shirts. I used to wear layers and give them away a layer at a time. This was my first introduction to life in Kenya.

Joan of Arc and the Dancing Swords

One of my friends had a dream, a real encouraging word for the season, saying Joan of Arc was around me. We had lots of visitations from Joan of Arc during meetings in Wales. In one such encounter my friend sensed that Deborah, from the Bible, was in the meeting. It seemed to her that I was like a warrior bride who sat on a horse, with a flaming sword in my hand. She said they were like jousting swords which danced around me like cherubim. Later that year I had an encounter where I went into the throne room and saw the cherubim. Interesting thing was that I was riding on the same horse, understanding the revelation that it was all about global connections. That is exactly what happened after that conference; I began to connect with other nations, which led me to go to Africa.

Alice in Wonderland

In another encounter in 2014, I was taken into a not visually very clear vision, but I knew I was in the Throne Room because, like Alice in Wonderland, initially my spirit was very, very, big and then my spirit shrunk and I went down a low, low, door in the floor. I could hear the pulsating of huge, great big wings above me and I could see through to the back of me and realised it was a Cherub. In the centre of the Cherub's chest was a huge ruby in the shape of a heart. Ruby red, it was emanating frequency almost like a kaleidoscope of red frequency.

As I turned to look at the Cherub, I felt a large furry brown animal walk past me and brush my left leg. I looked down and saw that it was a lion. He turned his head and looked back at me with massive brown whirlpool eyes and I slipped into the Eye of God.

The Lion of the tribe of Judah. Lion, ox, eagle, man, the four faces of the Cherubim. I was in the Lion. Instantly, in front of me, were two huge wings crossing over with eyes, eyes, eyes. I looked from the left to the right on each feather of the wings and the eyes followed me looking at me. It was scary! I was looking at one wing from left to right and right to left. In the middle of the right-hand wing, I noticed a blurred red eye which blinked at me. As I took a closer look it sucked me through the eye. Day and night I kept sinking back through the same vision, going through the red blurry eye.

Once the fur of the lion came past my leg, I remembered the peace and comfort. I reached down to stroke the Lion's fur. Abba. Papa, I remember thinking when the Lion looked back at me, "Just one look and I am wrecked by the soft brown eyes of love."

I had an overwhelming sense this blinking eye had to do with generational bloodline cleansing.

The Dread Champions

What a privilege it has been to travel the world with Justin Abraham and Stevie Mckie throughout the years. One trip that really stands out from the rest was in 2012. Once, in Africa, we stayed in a house overlooking the sea, high up on a cliff. Windows had screens over them to stop the cheeky monkeys from trying to get into the house. Justin gave up his bedroom for me because of the mosquitoes, but in the morning, he was covered in mosquito bites up and down his neck and arms with much swelling.

We went to a meeting that night and were amazed at the incredible goodness of God to us and at what He did at the meeting.

Afterwards, we went to a bakery and bought a whole lot of buns and were comfort-eating in the car.

Later Justin went into another realm. He started prophesying over me, "Jane Schroeder you are a Dread Champion, a Joan of Arc, you are a leader, you are a general." He called this forth from an expanded realm. As he spoke this, Stevie and I went with him into that realm. It wasn't about being taught or caught up together but was more about the precious time we spent together.

Bergville, South Africa

I was in South Africa in a place called Bergville. We were there with a guy called Wendell and we did a lot of street evangelism with his team and saw amazing things happen on the streets of Bergville. As we meandered through the market's narrow streets stopping to pray with different people there was a man with a very swollen left knee. We prayed once and nothing happened. The second time I felt swelling in his knee go down as I placed my hand on his knee. Just down the street, there was a young boy selling CDs. With our interpreter Wendell, he explained to us that the boy wanted a better standard of living for himself and his family. We prayed and his eyes began to flicker straight away with the presence of the Holy Spirit.

We didn't speak a word but waited on Holy Spirit, and instantly in front of our eyes in the Spirit, we saw him turn into a white eagle with fiery eyes. It was so clear to us that he had fiery eyes, a hooked beak and brown feathers on his head. Justin also testified saying he saw this boy as an eagle. And in broken Afrikaans, we told him he was a natural seer and left him with a beaming smile and a hope for his future. As I retell this story, I feel the presence of God and get so excited. I can tell from this energy that this is what I am supposed to be doing, going out to where the people are and bringing the love of my Father to them.

A woman who was part of a group of women, saw what we were doing and that people were getting healed so she shouted out, "I am a sorcerer, come and pray for me." We prayed for her, touched her feet and released joy, and we were speaking holy miracles, signs and wonders over their lives as healings were breaking out all over the place.

Stag on a hill - 13th September 2019
In one meeting, we were in a worship set praying for people who were lying all over the floor from the weight of the presence of God. I went up to a white South African woman and noticed her face appeared to me like that of the healing minister from the past named Kathryn Kuhlman, whose presence I was overwhelmed by at that moment. I

had this compulsion to blow my breath on the top of her head and hover my hand above her throat. The beauty of her shiny shimmering face was serene and spectacular. She looked exquisite. I took her by her hands and she sat up.

I was then called to share at a large meeting. I was really scared. In those days I hadn't done much speaking. Nowadays I still get a churning in my stomach but it is a little different than back then, when I was so nervous. Now it is because I just want to please my Father. As I looked beyond the crowd there was a big ball of bright light, which appeared to be associated with a ninety-year-old man named Neil. He was the great grandfather of the people that invited us to speak. I instantly was distracted by what I was sharing as I saw what he really looked like in the spirit in the kingdom realm.

I saw him as a large stag on a hill with massive antlers. He was strong and gracious, a bold leader. As he stood on the hill, the faithful stag shifted shape into the face of ABBA Father. DONE!

Quickly after this encounter I was back in the meeting and calling people into the realms of seeing, hearing, feeling and engaging in their destiny and their future.

African Safari

During that trip, I had the privilege of going on my first ever African Safari. It was a wee canoe trip. We saw giraffes, hippos and ostriches up close, and finished up a fantastic day in a farmhouse where we had amazing food and watched the sun go down on the beautiful moonlit African Safari skyline, which stretched out over the whole universe.

As we were going back from the Safari, I saw mountain ranges in the distance with streaks of fire coming down the mountainside as the sun set. As it went down it lit up the sky. It was bushfires.

A sacred dance of love, a wedding dance.

The theologians in the early church tried to describe this wonderful reality that we call Trinity. If any of you have ever been to a Greek wedding, you may have seen their distinctive way of dancing…it's called perichoresis. There are not two dancers, but at least three. They start to go in circles, weaving in and out in this very beautiful pattern of motion. They start to go faster and faster and faster, all the while staying in perfect rhythm and in sync with each other. Eventually, they are dancing so quickly (yet so effortlessly) that as you look at them, it just becomes a blur. Their individual identities are part of a larger dance. The early church fathers and mothers looked at that dance ([1]perichoresis) and said, "That's what the Trinity is like." It's a harmonious set of relationships in which there is mutual giving and receiving. This relationship is called love, and it's what the Trinity is all about. The perichoresis is the dance of love.

Co-crucified with Christ

One of the highlights of my trip was when Justin Abraham was talking about the co-crucified and he was so intoxicated in union with Christ that he slid down the lectern stand where he had

put his notes and held on to the lectern for about an hour. The presence of God was so strong. People lay out on the floor in union with God for hours and hours. The worship team was crashing on the floor as they could no longer stand under the weight and power of God's glory. Justin began to talk about the Song of Songs and the sacred dance of 1 Perichoresis. People lay on the floor "birthing" in the spirit, (Giving birth in the Spirit can be likened to the "travail" or "birthing"). Men and women of old would go through a kind of physical supernatural birthing in the presence of God.

This also works in prayer: We must persevere, as some strongholds and many blessings are only wrought through gut-wrenching, soul-searching prayer. When we travail in prayer, God hears the cries of His children. At the end of the meeting, the presence was so strong you could cut the atmosphere with a butter knife.

I began to drift into a visionary state. It was Jesus, as a beautiful horse. He put his mouth into my hands and I fed Him food. I could feel His breath and warm lips on my hands and then He nuzzled into my neck. It was Holy but creepy at the same time. I was weeping and crying. In fact, most of the meeting was weeping and crying. Justin was prostrate in the Spirit but clinging on to the cross at the front of the meeting room.

Then I heard horse's hooves. Jesus was actually a warrior horse.
I was aware of every detail, every hair of His coat. A big strong hand swooped below me and flung me onto the horse, and as I was compelled to wrap my hands around His waist physically, Jesus sat with me on the horse. He was two dimensional as the horse was Jesus and Jesus was riding the horse all at the same time.

1 PERICHORESIS - The divine Dance of the Trinity is a term referring to the relationship of the three persons of the Triune God, Father, Son and the Holy Spirit to one another.

I began to realise where we were was a place that was dark, cold and wet but I knew that being with Jesus I would be all right. As I drifted out of the vision and back into the reality of the room, there was a massive party fest. People dancing and waving flags and throwing water everywhere. That was normal for us in them days.

On our way to Durban, South Africa, we stopped to go to the toilet and grab a coffee. Three ladies sat outside. They offered me a cup of tea and I accepted the tea and as I began to sip, the presence of God went into one lady's body and began to heal her of pain. I didn't ask her and she didn't tell me, but she got healed while I drank the tea they offered. I knew the woman was healed as I felt it through my gut feeling, Holy Spirit nudging. I call it discernment, because her face lit up full of joy.

William Branham's Crusade, Durban

Little did we know that there were some surprises waiting for us here. One night when we went to bed, I began to ascend into the heavenly realm.

I had tucked away in my suitcases one of William Branham's fabulous books, which I couldn't put down. I especially loved the part about the angelic encounter he had when he visited Durban. I was ploughing through that very chapter not knowing the area where we were staying was near the actual race course where 70,000 people met when he preached.

Stevie and I decided to look up the racecourse, Greyville Racecourse, and go there. On arrival, a massive mosque was set up to shout out a call to their prayers. I was annoyed that this place that once had been filled with the Glory of the Lord, salvation, healing and worship to God had lost its spiritual position. I climbed up onto a grandstand and we took a video. I did not know that I was standing at the very spot William Branham had stood until we saw a photo later. The video went viral on YouTube.

We went to a place called uShaka Marine World and as we wandered around all afternoon, we felt the really strong presence of an angel. With the overflow of the afternoon's angelic engagement into the evening church meeting, we prayed for a lady that had carpal tunnel neck pain and a seized shoulder. Wow! She didn't ask for prayer for herself but for her son who had an accident in church. He banged his head and got a blood clot with swelling on the back of his head, yet she was healed during this prayer.

The angel that was following us all day we now believe was "Watcher," Branham's angel, which is why all the healings were breaking out. What I am trying to say is that we really need to learn to partner with the angelic. They surround us 24/7.

Perfect Government
10/10/12. The number 10 means government and the number 12 means perfect government. On this day I had a visit from one of John Paul Jackson's leaders who stayed in my little cottage on the hill for one night. He was amazed as in the middle of my lounge he saw a very large tree with blue and green leaves, leaves of revelation. He perceived this by the Spirit in the Kingdom realms. We began to realise the tree in the middle of my lounge was an oak tree.

Isaiah 61:2 (NASB)
To grant those who mourn in Zion,
Giving them a garland instead of ashes,
The oil of gladness instead of mourning,
The cloak of praise instead of a disheartened spirit.
So they will be called oaks of righteousness,
The planting of the Lord, that He may be glorified.

Healing for their Hearts

We began to realise in Durban, South Africa, that we were praying for lots of healing for people's hearts, which was very different from other cities in South Africa.

One very special night on the 4th of October 2012, staying in a house overlooking the beach, we could see the stunning crest of waves on the rocks below the beach. We even saw whales swimming by. During our visit a strange presence descended into the living room, as we were all sitting together after a really busy day, praying for people and doing meetings. Justin began to prophesy. There was the "Bench of Three" of us that sat over the region for that short time that we were there. In those days we didn't know about the "Bench of Three," or the Courts of Heaven, the only way we could describe it was that the terror and fear of The Lord enveloped us for two hours. We would see the "dread champions" arise in the nation and we would begin to see in the natural and the external realms of nature, earthquakes as a sign and wonder of what Yahweh was going to bring on the earth. We are in that time now... volcanoes in Iceland and earthquakes have magnified and increased!

Offences come and go
by M.M. van Rensburg

Offences come and go
thoughts crashing on the shore of my
mind
thoughts of people, things
they come and go rhythmically
then my ear is cut off and suddenly i
realise i am a king and the offence is gone
and all i know is the crashing of the ocean
of the love of a Saviour who gave
all died for all of my offences that make
me sick and deaf

CHAPTER SEVEN
Family

There is absolutely no one who can replace doing life with and being the sandpaper as well as the smooth honey goo, as your flesh and blood family and those who marry into it. You love 'em, hate 'em, and forgive 'em and certainly find it hard to live a long way from them or without them. I have a rambunctious, loving family and oh wow, have we had some crazy experiences over the years. Enjoy getting to know them a little bit in these, my favourite stories, shared in life with them.

If Jesus came to my house!

I was seven years old and on a rainy evening sat shaking in my gum-boots in a little red minivan, after practising my four lines for the up-and-coming Sunday School anniversary.

My parents would each year attend by sitting at the back of Waverton Village Methodist Chapel. On that hot summer's evening, it was to hear my brother Nigel, sister Jennifer and I sing choruses and recite verses from a children's book *"If Jesus Came To My House"*.

My mum was so proud of my sister and I in our new summer dresses that she had spent hours sewing on her "Joneses" hand sewing machine which she bought after saving up what she could from her housekeeping allowance for the whole year.

The sliding door of the van opened right next to where I was sitting. An elderly lady, Mrs Mills, stood holding a brown paper bag and handed it to me. Embarrassed and painfully shy I took it home to show my mum the gift I had been given. Inside was the book of a seven-year-old boy's story about his imagination, and the dream of Jesus visiting him. I was the same age and height as him!

Fast forward seven years, in my bedroom. There were beautiful frosted pattern shapes sketched on my windows, more frost inside the window than outside. Shivering with the cold and short of breath, my dad would rub oil on my throat and chest to help ease the asthma panic attacks in the middle of the night and he would still have to be up at the crack of dawn to cycle miles to work.

One night I awoke in the familiar panic to see a visible misty cloud just in front of me. Moses dropped out of the cloud right in front of my eyes. The story of Moses had always been a delight to me.

If Jesus Came to my House
by Joan Gale Thomas

If Jesus came to my house
and knocked upon the door
I'm sure I'd be more happy
than I've ever been before.

If Jesus came my house
I'd like him best to be
about the age that I am
and about the height of me.

I'd run down stairs to meet Him,
the door I'd open wide
and would say to Jesus Oh,
won't you come inside?

I'd offer Him my rocking chair,
it's such a comfy seat
and on the kitchen fender
He should warm His little feet.

My kitten and my puppy dog
would sit beside His chair
and they would be as pleased as me at
seeing Jesus there.

Then I would put the kettle on
to make a cup of tea,

and we would be as happy
and as friendly as could be...

I'd show him all the places
that are nicest in the house
The hole behind the stairs
Where I pretend I am a mouse.

The little window up above
Where I can stand and see
The people down below
Yet they can't see me.

Then I think I'd show him
The corner in the hall
Where am sometimes rather frightened
By the shadows on the wall.

I always have to hurry
When going passed at night
But hand in hand with Jesus
Am perfectly alright.

I'd show him round the garden
And ask him please to bless
The seeds that I had planted
The mustard and the cress

My Dad

My dad lived in a little village called Waverton and knew everybody. He was chairman of the local council and was a strong Methodist and really loved the Lord. All his life Dad had never locked his house or his car.

Dad loved gardening and he had an allotment for all of his grown-up life. He gave away veggies and flowers, but he had a little box at the back of his door where people could make donations. As the village changed and more people came to live there, he noticed money was going out of his money box. This deeply troubled my dad because while he appreciated the donations towards his expenses, he would gladly give the vegetables away so he really wanted to get to the bottom of the money missing from his money box.

He devised a little plan where he dug a little safe into the brickwork. Contributors would put the money between the crack of the bricks which fed to the little money box. This system worked ok until the money box was dug up and stolen.

Dad's next strategy was to have people put the money in his letterbox. Seasons came and went. Beautiful broccoli, sprouts and rows and rows of beautiful Sweet William cut flowers.

Spring came and we broke out hundreds of plants to sell. Begonias, Verbenas, French Marigolds, every flower you could imagine. In the front garden he grew lettuce where there should have been flowers. Every year Dad won the village competition called "Chester In Bloom."

The winter came again and then the spring and once

again money started disappearing from his letterbox! At this time Dad became very friendly with the local village bobby. He spoke at the local village community meetings and told village tales and funny stories. He would give away his secret gardening hints for the best carrots and flowers. Even a television crew filmed him for a gardening programme.

My dad had many roles and was a well-known character in the community. He was known as Mr Mole, the village mole catcher, Johnny Jones or Mr Man-web because he worked for the local electrical board. He rode his bike everywhere and no one would ever guess my dad was devising a plan to catch the thief.

One evening, at dusk, my husband and I went to visit him. I couldn't open the front gate. The gate felt like it was on a string so my husband said, "Let's jump over the hedge." I fell over a tripwire and was furious. I told my dad the village policeman would find out about this and my dad said that the village bobby already knew. I was worried he would get into trouble as he had the front yard booby trapped.

I went home and went to bed worried about this situation and praying. I phoned him the next day. The next morning there was blood on the letter box and on the front step. Apparently, Dad had put a rat trap in the letterbox! He knew about catching anything, even a small change thief. He never had to do anything ever again and no money ever got stolen again.

Years ago, we found out who had stolen the money. Being

a local hairdresser, I learned our small change thief was not a local boy but a naughty boy who sometimes stayed with his grandmother. One day when I was cutting her hair, she told me a story about her grandson hurting his fingers. I pieced the evidence together but didn't say anything to her. That was my dad, a country boy at heart who was a bit of a vigilante. Anyway, that was my dad, a minx — fun but naughty.

Reality of Relationships and How It Really Is

I met my husband in a nightclub. I was sitting at a bar as was often my custom chatting to a load of girls and the moment I clapped eyes on him I thought, "You know, I like him." He was tall, blonde and German. The real Rob was shy, he wasn't a big drinker but he loved his home and his family. It was definitely a divine appointment because a couple of weeks later we saw him again in a nightclub. There were other women chatting with him during the evening but at the end of the night, as I was leaving, he asked if he could meet me for coffee. We agreed to meet outside the local Job Centre the next day because, at the time we met, Rob was looking for work and, in those days, we didn't have mobile phones so we needed somewhere to connect.

The next day I nearly didn't go as I was so nervous. I decided the next best thing was to take my mum with me. My sister had just gotten married and my mum and I decided to pick up the
photographs of the wedding before my arranged meeting with Rob at the Job Centre. We went into the Job Centre and my Mum asked, "What are we doing here?" (My mum didn't know that we were meeting Rob there), so I just said, "We are going for a cuppa tea and a scone with raspberry

jam at Marks and Spencer." Even though Rob was surprised to see my mum he was happy to join both of us for tea.

Rob was the youngest son of three sons. His father was German and his mother was British. As we sat enjoying our cup of tea and raspberry jam scones, my mum and I looked at the photographs of my sister's wedding that we had just picked up. We showed some of the photos to Rob and he recognised the best man at the wedding as his brother's best friend! He also knew many other people in the wedding photographs. And so our romance began with my mum, my sister's wedding photographs and Devonshire Tea at the famous Marks and Spencer.

Rob and I were courting on and off for years. At one stage I moved away from Chester to Bristol, for work, so the distance ended the relationship for a while, but love has a way of bringing you back together. Eventually, I moved back to Chester and became self- employed as a hairdresser. Rob and I got married within a year of my return to Chester.

One night we were asleep in our room. I started to have dreams of German prisoners of war, persecution and torture. I already knew I could see in both realms but this is when it really began to bother us. I sat up in bed and started praying. Standing in front of me was a huge being with a scythe looking at me from another realm. There were also huge snakes coming towards me. In my half-asleep state I was kicking and fighting the snakes but I must have turned myself around in the bed and had been kicking my husband's head and he was covered with blood. It was then that I knew that I needed help understanding my dreams and seeing things in different realms before it

121

became a problem for us.

We eventually went back to sleep and the next day when Rob went to work the lads could not stop laughing and asking him how the catfights with his new wife were going. The lads all knew me because all of us associated with the electricity company my husband worked at used to go to parties together.

The Lord was so kind because the next year was the year I met my best friend, Rona Scott, whom the Lord had told that she would help me but I didn't know that at the time.

Within a year, as a mobile hairdresser, I went to perm Elaine's beautiful long curly hair. I had done her hair many times and didn't know, over a year before this, that the Lord had told her to pray for me. Halfway through the perm I began to cry. Elaine was panicking when I started crying as she was afraid that I would forget to take the curlers out of her hair, leaving a frizzy perm. I took the perm curlers out and as soon as I finished her hair Elaine and her daughter took me to the top of their three-story home to pray for me. They didn't know that just that week I had a diagnosis of pre-cancer cells in my body and would need extensive treatment.

As soon as they started to pray, I felt electricity in my left arm. I didn't know what was going on at the time but my understanding now is that I was baptised in the Holy Spirit. There was so much I didn't understand at the time but this was the beginning of a
journey of recognising that I was a 'Seer' and how to see in the Spirit as the Lord showed me. After this prayer, Elaine suggested I pray with Rona and a few others at a

place called The Olive Branch. The day came for me to go to see this lovely counselling group, The Olive Branch. My car wouldn't start and my friend's car broke down but we eventually got there. We were very determined.

I arrived and filled in what they called an "occult form" that asked what spiritual things I might have been involved with in the past. Then I sat on the floor, (I don't remember a thing), for five hours. They had other people booked in two hourly time slots and had to turn them away at the door. The Lord had told Rona it was not
going to be an easy journey but she had to love me unconditionally. I used to swear at them and everything but they never stopped loving me.

During the five-hour prayer session, one of the ladies had her hand on the door because as the demons were being released from me, she was terrified. I always knew from a teenager that I could see something in my eyes when I looked in the mirror but didn't know what it was so would dismiss it. This day was life-changing for me. Exhausted, I returned home and in a couple of weeks they said they would like to see me again to follow up on how I was. Once again, I was at The Olive Branch for hours and hours dealing with issues like shame, anger and forgiveness. We had gotten rid of the big boulders in the first session and now we were dealing with smaller blockages. These guys were amazingly patient and loving but also firm. Rona used to look at me and even with my eyes shut I could see like two burning fires in her eyes. When I was with Elaine, I felt like I was with a mother; protected and looked after.

Holy Spirit, Paraclete

One night, cooking dinner for my husband, newly married and in our new home, I picked up the food for the plate and all of a sudden, the whole room was like seeing ten films at the cinema.

I didn't understand it at the time but now I know it was an encounter in many dimensions at one time. My husband took me, curled up in a huddle in the front seat of our car, to Rona's house where she was hosting a small group meeting. I was so "out of it" I couldn't even sit properly in the car. Rona apologised to the group and went with Elaine to her house with Rob and I. Rob wasn't even a Christian but he loved me dearly and took me.

The moment I walked into Elaine's house I hid under the table like a small frightened child. A voice like a six-year-old came out of me. Rona and Elaine hopped under the table with me. I was having a flashback of a six-year old memory and we realised the Lord was shining a torch on my life so I could be healed. This began the transformation of many memories that had affected my heart and my soul. Rona is still my best friend to this day.

I began to learn how to pray and could pray for my husband in a deep way. The main thing that I learned about at that time was the person of Holy Spirit. The Greek word Paraclete *(παράκλητος)*, occurring five times in the Gospel of John in the New Testament commonly refers to the Holy Spirit and is translated as "advocate", "counsellor or helper", "to come alongside" and the Holy Spirit certainly did that for me. The Holy Spirit came alongside me and taught me so many things.

The work of the Holy Spirit

The work of Holy Spirit within us, awakening us until we are Oceans, Rivers of Oil, Life, Water, Fire upon us, with us, in us, full of Joy, Bliss, Ecstasy, we emerge in His love through yielding and surrender. We are dialled in every day into the goodness of God's Spirit.

Nehemiah 9:20 and *Psalm 143:10* God's good Spirit teaches us in

all of God's goodness. God's good gifts to us are for helping us in the present. Amazing reality! We are not alone in this world. Christ's very own Spirit is within us and with us to work all things out for our good.

Ephesians3:14, 'You were marked in Him with a seal, the promised Holy Spirit who is a deposit.

Comforting Symphony song

The Lord showed me something through a song called *Symphony* by Zara Larsson. Here are some of the lyrics.

"I just want to be part of your symphony, symphony.

Will you hold me tight and don't let go, I am holding tight, I'll let go.

Every healing, every melody is timeless. And now you are gone. I can't find a key without you. Your song is on repeat, I am dancing to your heartbeat."

This is a song Sam played over and over following the death of his father. Sam would play this song on repeat as it brought comfort to his grieving heart. Sam felt he couldn't find the key of life without his dad. The Lord was showing me it was His symphony, not our symphony, of sound. He showed me His heart for us as I spent a whole afternoon listening repeatedly to the symphony. It wrecked me. The Lord showed me every sound and frequency He makes is timeless, part of His universal symphony. If I am a part, so is everyone else, vibrating in the frequency of God. Clever, isn't it, what the Lord does.

Ruthie and Jay's Journey - by Ruth Merryweather

On another warm sunny afternoon, my dad stopped off in Walmart car park to meet a lad, skinhead Jay. After a two-and-a-half-year, long-distance romance, we finally were together forever. Five years ago, in a conference, we were learning how to speak to each other through the thoughts and intent of our hearts by engaging and holding our family in our hearts. We did a little activation by imagining a room in our homes. Mine was my kitchen. I saw my mum in an apron with lots of children surrounding her, teaching them cooking skills, sewing, and household chores. I noticed, through the open door from the kitchen, that my dad was digging in the ground in the garden, then the vision ended and I was back in the room. I could see the children's faces and features clearly, and knew in an instant they were my future grandchildren, the parents, my sons and daughters.

Ruth's Story

Fast forward a couple of years and I found myself awakened from my slumber on the other side of the world in Mildura, North West Victoria, Australia, to a live-feed Facebook gender reveal. Yes, my daughter and son-in-law were expecting a beautiful baby boy, Little did we know that through the whole pregnancy, Ruthie would be and feel sick even though her health checks were perfect. As the birth approached, the world changed in a day as country after country went into lockdown over the Coronavirus.

Written by Ruth

My mum was about to be promoted to nanny but not before I was twelve days overdue. I was still working, knocking concrete boulders which were from a recent family creative project of an unusually large garden shed or should I say on site storage, with a sledge hammer.

The day arrived and my amazing husband dropped me off at the hospital for inducement. Our emotions ran high with excitement and anxiety during most of my labour without my two birthing partners, Jay and mum, being able to be by my side because of the coronavirus health restrictions in the hospitals. The nursing staff and midwives were so kind and helpful. I spent most of the first part of my first labour and birth of our baby boy physically on my own with mum and Jay part-time on Face-Time video, encouraging me.

At home, I knew mum and her crazy intercessors had been praying day and night for our safety, angelic protection and heaven invading earth in a blanket of love, sweet love. After a good nineteen hours labour the pain had become super intense and I really needed Jay to join me with comfort after being told around 2.30pm in the afternoon I was still only 4cm dilated. My waters needed to break while a bed on the labour ward awaited me. By the time 5pm came and went, I had not moved to the labour ward where I would at least have some gas and air to support me. I could take no more, I phoned Jay and started crying and Jay was desperate to be at my side.

While mum was walking the doggies talking to Papa God,

doing her thing as she tells it, she went into a vision where she laid hands on my tummy, calling forth Arthur baby boy. She immediately saw the baby's body was blue, starved of oxygen. At first she thought it was to do with a song she had been singing to him in my tummy — my womb, "Blued eyed baby boy, king noble king."

On arriving at our home, mum called a good friend of ours, a retired midwife for support, trying not to show how worried she was about the progression of the birth. Elaine and mum prayed together then suddenly the phone call came for hubby to join at the hospital.
Mum dropped Jay at the hospital, drove home and she said *shalom* and the peace that passes all understanding wrapped itself around her. Then Sam, my brother, and her power-hosed the cars. Yes, they really did!

Precious Family Written by Jane

At 6.15pm a text arrived with the most beautiful photograph of my precious Ruthie, Jay and baby Arthur, after an emergency C-section. No sooner had Ruthie been moved into the labour ward they broke her waters as promised hours before. They realised that the cord was wrapped not only around Arthur's arm, but his neck as well. As soon as Jay had arrived at the hospital to be with Ruthie, they gowned him up and he was greeted to the loud sound of a baby crying. Arthur was out of Ruthie's belly; such joy and relief filled the airways. A 9lb 2oz wide-eyed baby snuggled in for his first cuddles with mummy and daddy Merryweather. From then on, all the pregnancy vomiting left immediately. Ruthie, starving and hungry, returned home within twenty-four hours flat.

Weird times we live in. Normally a midwife would be doing home visits for the first five days, but nope, coronavirus put paid to that one. The two bunnies settled down together in the morning light of day with harmony, love, peace and joy, in awe and wonder of what they had both knitted together in the womb. I was so grateful for the naturally supernatural grace, but grace freely given from a faithful God and in the depths of my heart I truly know that you, Yahweh, have become my Shield.

What have we learnt from this situation, I ask you?

Psalm 18:2
The Lord is my rock and fortress and my deliverer, My God my rock, in whom I take refuge. My shield and the horn of my salvation, my stronghold. But in the depths of my heart, I truly know that You Yahweh, have become my Shield; You take me and surround me with yourself. Your glory covers me continually. You lift high my head when I bow low in shame

Grandad & Sam's Stories

Sidney Two and Three Ferrets
My grandad Johnny Jones, alias "Man-web Jones," was named after he cycled everywhere on his bike before the electrical company had vans. Me and granddad one day, when I was a lad, hid a live ferret inside his trench coat and thought, wouldn't it be fun to let it run loose around the lounge where my nanny was sitting reading her newspaper. She screamed with fright, "Get Sidney out of here!" as Grandad popped the ferret down his trouser leg with a wide-open grin on his face.

The Mole Catcher

Grandad was an amazing teacher in ways of countryside living. From a young boy he was raised in a small village and he knew the times and seasons of the land, from hunting and trapping wild animals to knowing what wild nuts and berries to forage to keep his family fed. We would walk miles setting traps to catch rabbits and moles. Moles can be a complete nuisance because it is thought they can lift twenty times their body weight. They can lift patio slabs up where the leaves have piled up overnight. Local friends and farmers would invite us to catch them as humanely as possible. The traps we used had been passed down through the generations. One long day we walked across fields to bring back our spoils, to of course sneak up on Nanny and launch them through the lounge door in her direction, making her jump out of her skin and scream, "John, get them out of here!" Much to us youngster's delight.

I grew up eating whatever was caught off the land, from all different kinds of fish, rabbit, hare, pheasant, road kill sheep and even holy pigeons from the local church bell tower where from the age of fourteen, I learnt campanology bell ringing. As my sister and I weren't quite tall enough we stood on wooden boxes to catch the sally.

Dreaming with Abba God
Ruth Schroeder's Dream of The Lion
This is a dream my daughter Ruth had when she was 22 years old after an unsettling time of moving from Chester to Risca, Newport, South Wales.

My daughter dreamt of a miniature animal about the size of a small deer or fox. It had small little legs with spots on its body. At first, she thought the creature was a fox because of the tail and the legs but when she revisited the dream, she realised half of this creature was like a lion and leopard with spots and an orange colour. We later discovered they breed a lion with a leopard, a hybrid called a leopon, (A portmanteau of leopard and lion). It's the offspring of a male leopard and female lion. The head of the animal is similar to that of a lion, while the rest of the body carries similarities to leopards.

We had just moved into an old-fashioned house with a log burner and the lion came into the kitchen and walked on the worktops. It walked through our lounge and upstairs to my daughter's bed while she was sleeping. As she woke up it looked into her face. Ruth said the lion then looked at me but I wasn't aware that the lion was there.

The next thing Ruthie remembers is that the animal went down the stairs and began walking on the kitchen worktop and then out the kitchen door. The lion walked out of the garden, straight through the back fence and went to join five lionesses on the mountain. Our back garden was an open garden stretching out to the mountain range behind our house, which is how it was in real life. The kitchen was below the level of the mountain. There was a small fence between fields, normally full of bleating sheep. In the dream an archway was created with two palest pink, soft blush Avalanche rose trees in front of the arch. (This is Ruth's favourite flower. She had trained at a Florist's college and she actually had the same type of flower for her wedding years later! The Lord knows these things. It is only now years later we understand what was going on in the dream.)

Ruth and I believe God himself visited her that night. We felt God's blessing on our move and were able to face the challenges knowing God was in it and He would provide and care for us in this new season. He was in my daughter's heart.

Pirates, Monks and Nuns

As we were preparing to put together this diary my daughter and I were discussing what stories to include. My daughter wondered if I remembered when we used to go with Justin Abraham and David Vaughan, in the days of Emerge Wales, and dress up as pirates, monks and nuns in the streets. The purpose of dressing as monks and nuns was to honour the Celtic faith. The purpose of dressing as pirates was to hijack people into paradise.

About fifteen to twenty of us would go on the streets in Guilford, London and take drummers with us, who would play drums and dance. The joy was unbelievable. People would get saved and healed and would queue for prophecies. We would connect with shopkeepers, police, everyone and anyone on the streets. One day one of the drummers, Martin, who had long hair with dreadlocks, started to break dance and do crazy acrobatics, and people's inhibitions left them and they started to join in with him.

We had a megaphone and would do crazy things like pretending we were taking a magic carpet going into heaven or breast stroking in an imaginary swimming pool. People would pass by and join in or just fall in the glory that was created. We would see healing and miracles.

We did this thing called "free buzz", where we would ask people to put their hands out and we would put our hands out hovering on top of theirs and they could feel the glory of the Holy Spirit and His presence.

We used to sing one song with these lyrics, "The roof, the roof, the roof is on fire. If you want to party then take it up higher." Catholics would ask if we were mocking them and we would say no, we love them and are honouring them and they would get deeply touched. During these events, we would often experience massive outbreaks of the goodness of God for hours.

'Glory invasion needs no persuasion, it is the glory invasion.'
One evening when we all went back to our accommodation between the daytime street ministry and the night-time meetings, I had come back from a really busy day to find my daughter was suddenly ill, slumped with her head leaning against the toilet and she proceeded to pass out. The girl we were staying with, Grace, was a nurse and she took my daughter's pulse and said we needed to call the paramedics. I said, "Just before you do that let's phone Justin." It was about 1am in the morning and very late but I knew in my heart he would answer the phone for me. Justin woke from his sleep at my call and I told him the situation. He said he would pray immediately and he put the phone down. We sat on the bathroom floor really worried. Soon we felt the really strong presence of Justin in the bathroom. Unknown to us he sat up in bed and began praying for Ruth and he said there was like a wheel in the Spirit and he turned the wheel. We knew the exact time in the Spirit when this had occurred as my daughter Ruth began to instantly recover and slept through the night. When she awoke the next day, she could not even remember being ill! Stevie told me afterwards that one time Justin went to Stevie all night and prayed for Stevie and in turn Stevie prayed for a woman who was dying of cancer and she was healed.

CHAPTER EIGHT

Mr Su and Other Stories

I think you will probably laugh and gasp at the incredulousness of some of the following stories. The thing with the freedom of the Holy Spirit is that I never know what to expect in my life, so I am always open and ready for the unexpected move of God through His Holy Spirit, keeping my heart, mind and eyes of my Spirit open to the exciting experiences that He wants to show me or for me to experience. Some are for my growth, some for other people's healing and growth and some for my sheer love relationship with Him.

Mr Su The Chinese Restaurant Owner who lived in Chinatown in Liverpool, UK

One night I had a dream that I was a big yellow JCB digger, a bulldozer, and I was digging up the ground. I awoke thinking, "This is a weird dream." That morning, when I went to church, there was a young family waiting for me. They said that the Lord had told them, "I did 'dead'!" They went on to say that during that week the woman's dad had died and he was in the mortuary in the hospital in Liverpool. They asked if I would go with them to pray for her dead father.

I was a little bit surprised at this request because no one had ever asked me anything like this before but during the morning service I had a confirmation to go and pray. I wasn't sure what to do as my husband didn't go to church and I didn't know what to do with our small children. For the first time that morning, I was called to go up to the front of the church during the meeting and give prophetic words. Many people were healed. There was a very strong atmosphere of the presence of God. After the meeting, my friend offered to drop my children back to their dad's home. I didn't tell him what I was going to do because I knew he would say no.

I had never before seen a dead body and decided to go on an instant fast. No food, no water and constantly asking the Lord if He was sure that He wanted me to do this. So the couple, whose father had died, and I drove to the morgue and the daughter of the dead man was describing to me what he might look like. I was just scared.

When we got to the hospital we had to wait for hours. I was even more anxious about Rob, my husband wondering where the heck I was. Eventually, we went to a beautiful underground room. A large drawer opened up and there lay the dead man. I sensed the Lord say I was to breathe up the dead man's nostrils. In my heart I said, "No way!" He looked so beautiful and peaceful, in his best suit and I found out he had been embalmed. He had died from a heart attack. We did pray about raising from the dead but I was too scared to breathe up his nostrils, (I would do it now but not then). When we had finished praying, I said goodbye to my friend. She thanked me and we went home.

My husband was furious. Days later we got the funeral date but it was while my son was in his last year of primary school and it was a school day. I didn't tell my husband and snuck him out of school for the afternoon in his school uniform and drove, in the pouring rain, to what I didn't know was going to be a massive funeral at the Chinese church in Liverpool. My lovely son Sam, who knows to show respect and give up his chair, stood by the wall while I had a seat. I didn't know at the time when we took our places that he would be standing right at the head of the embalmed man's body. The next thing I knew Sam had disappeared out the door. I was blocked in against the wall and could not get out to find out where my naughty boy had disappeared too. It was a long service and many people spoke and I was very anxious not knowing where my son had gone. At the end of the service, we all went up to the coffin and many kissed the dead man's head and that is when I saw my son. He was in the hearse having a ride on the electric belt riding in and out of the hearse. We were invited to the wake but I could not handle all the questions from my inquisitive Sam.

I hadn't planned to tell my husband about this adventure but eventually I had to come clean because of course, my son told his dad how he had been in a hearse and how he had seen a dead man who looked alive! My husband continued to bring this topic up over the years as he would complain about his wife taking a young boy to a funeral with an open casket with a dead, embalmed body. My son and I used to laugh. We thought it was funny. To this day we laugh about things nobody else does.

Another Woman who Died
I went to an evening meeting of Tommy Tenny at the Vineyard Church in Manchester. He was doing a lovely presentation about Hadassah, based on his book *"One night with the King"*. It was a wonderful evening.

As I left to go to an open car park, I noticed a woman lying on the ground. She had the same tight curly hair that I had. There were people gathered around her and her car was next to mine. Without thinking I opened the passenger's side of her car and leaned over the seat where she lay on the ground just outside the driver's door. I found myself instantly in travail in the Spirit. A professional nurse, whom I had only met briefly before, was trying to resuscitate her and people had phoned for an ambulance, but I did not know this at the time. As I prayed, I heard the Lord say, "Tell them to let her go". I didn't verbalise this at the time.

The lady lying on the ground was in her 50s. I found out weeks later that the Lord took her at her word. While I was praying for this woman, leaning through the passenger door, nobody saw my face, they only saw my hand. After praying for the woman, I snuck out and hid around the corner until I had the composure to go back to my car. My friend Mark came out and hugged me exclaiming, "Jane you are alive!" They thought I was dead on the floor as the woman and I had similar curly hair. That became a standing joke at the church that I had "risen from the dead."

What I found out a few weeks later when I spoke to her friends at the Healing Rooms and asked after her, they said that when Tommy Tenny had shared about *One Night with the King",* the story of Esther, the lady had said, "Take my life, Lord" and she had repeated to her one friend that she just wanted the Lord to take her home, but I don't think her friends believed her at the time. She passed away in the car park, before even getting home. I was weeping and crying that the Lord had taken her at her word.

Through these experiences of death, I felt like the Lord was preparing me for what was to come, to not be afraid to speak out and say what the Lord was telling me to do because I was so painfully shy at that time.

The Turquoise Gem Dream

In another dream, Todd Bentley appeared to me holding a turquoise gemstone in his right hand as big as the palm of his hand. He pushed the gemstone into the left side of my chest and it burned. I could feel the flesh burning and I actually felt pain. To my surprise, within a couple of years, I got an invitation to minister with Todd in India.

At first I thought gemstones were to do with the gemstones on the priest's chest but when in a meeting in Scotland, with a **tallit** over my head in worship, a rod of crystal (I thought it was a bolt of lightning), was dancing around and I had to chase it to grasp it. When I grabbed it in my hand the stone placed in my chest began to glow and burn and burst out of my chest and went straight to the top of the rod. The moment it set itself in the setting of the rod, blue lightning came out of it. I asked the Lord what was that and he said, "That is how I speak to you telepathically through the blue DNA strand."

This happened in winter. I was driving my car on a lonely road in the dark and the DNA strand came out of my stomach and sat on my lap as I drove. The Lord said it was His DNA; a three strand cord. I have heard people say that is how the Lord communicates to some people in heaven through these three strand cords of twisted, woven together DNA, sonic boom, His thought speed, faster than the speed of light. Symphony, frequency and sound. Love this so much.

Hyderabad, India and the dead boy

I was with Todd Bentley in Hyderabad, India three years ago and a little boy was brought into the meeting, draped in a beautiful velvet purple cloth. His parents brought him to the front of the meeting, opened the cloth and asked us to pray. He had died that morning of lung cancer, drowning in his own fluids at nine years of age. I did not know the child had died as I was busy praying for others, but Todd called me out to pray. I prayed and wept for two hours and I know others prayed as well, while Todd sat crossed-legged on the floor comforting the mother. The child did not live.

This sounds nuts, but the Lord always says to me, "Practice, practice, practice!" All these experiences build confidence, bravery, single- mindedness, faithfulness etc. A lot of people say to me that I am really faithful but the Lord forged it with circumstances and how I dealt with them. I think we have a massive God who is constantly cheering us on and saying to us, "Come on, come on, you can do it, the Lord your God is with you!"

The Glory Cloud

This was incredible! I was in a meeting with a small group of people, praying and seeking the Lord for the country of Wales. During the worship time I was compelled to put both hands into the air and it felt like I was reaching into a cloud. As I reached up, the cloud became a glory cloud and when I put my hands into the cloud, they were covered in gold dust but when I pulled my hands out of the cloud there was none. With a thought, I remembered Bill

Johnson who had at least twenty-nine visitations of a glory cloud and I thought, "Why not us, why not now?" I just thought it, I didn't pray it.

Instantly, in a vision, Bill Johnson appeared on something like a raised platform in a high place in the air in front of me. His shirt was really nice and reminded me of a cloud. He had his Texan hat on and said, "Tell them all in the meeting to put their hands into the cloud." I was like, "What?" Unbeknown to me Rachael, one of the singers also saw what was happening in the Spirit Kingdom realm of heaven. I opened my eyes and the microphone that she was holding was in front of me, so I began to speak out what I was seeing in the visionary state. We all put our hands in the air and into the cloud. I could see, just above the building, a massive cloud that remained there for the whole night and we were all covered with gold dust.

A couple of months later I was in an airport in Singapore about to fly home and I started to weep and cry because I felt that same presence again. My friend interpreted this visitation and said, of
of course, Bill Johnson represents the Father, Abba, and The Lord wants to "father" us not only individually but as nations, regions, villages and towns. He is drawing us into the "cloud of all knowing", the cloud of His Presence, into the presence of the Father, Abba. Even as we were speaking about this vision, the presence of God came down.

Disappearance - 20th March 2014
I was driving along Newport Road to work, as a special needs support worker, on the way to pick up a client with Cerebral Palsy. I was listening to some worship music about

the only pure in heart would see God, when I felt, the only way to describe it, a "Scary Glory" presence in my car.

My body and Spirit started to expand differently than I had ever experienced before. Recently I had gone through some personal accusations, unable to defend myself. It felt a bit like lying flat on the ground while a large steam roller slowly rolled over my body and then off the edge of a cliff. I was having a grumpy moment as it should have been my day off from work but my daughter had injured her back and I felt the need to cover her shift, servant- hearted.

I had spent months checking my heart, repenting, and going lower in love and humility. Yet again I found myself asking Papa God to pierce my heart with forgiveness and a supernatural love for people as I pondered the sacrificial love Jesus bore on the cross once and for all. Without any warning, I saw in midair a floating Crucified Christ with his head bowed, bleeding, dying for me and my sins, how could I not forgive!

Uncontrollable weeping followed, by this time the car I was driving expanded like a giant truck, and the bottom of the car swelled up like a HoverCraft floating on air. A red shiny car had pulled up next to me at the traffic lights and my thoughts concerned me. What would people think if they noticed me weeping and crying in the car next to them? The reflection looking back at me from the red car indicated the wheels of my car weren't touching the ground or road and at the same time I felt weird like I was turning over and over in the clouds, and I had never felt like this before. I looked down at my left hand.

It flashed disappearing twice, then I looked at my left

knee, the same thing was happening. I panicked a bit but managed to drive five minutes further down the road to pick up my client. I was so freaked out I phoned a friend who had recently half disappeared in front of her mum's eyes while washing and drying dishes in their kitchen! She prayed for me, laughing down the phone. I had dropped my iPhone the day before and cracked the screen and unbeknown to me had called multiple people too.

Weeping and laughing together at once, as well as praying about being present in both heavenly and earthly realms, all at the same time trying to bring my Spirit back into my body. Interestingly I could see in the Spirit Kingdom Realms as my body was lying down. It was like my Spirit had sat up and levitated.

By now a taxi came to pick up my client in her wheelchair and I, to go to our singing and dance class. My client needed to be held up to walk and was very frail and thin. Whipping, swirling, the angels danced around us as we giggled and played together for hours as there seemed to be a supernatural strength on us both. Then it was time for the taxi to arrive to take us into town for lunch. The taxi driver was full of questions about why we were so full of joy and excitement. We introduced him to Jesus!

I left the taxi and pushed my client towards the elevator up to our local department store cafe. A lady was already inside the lift so I leaned to press the elevator button but before I had the chance, BAM, we were on the second floor within seconds! This was so unusual as it normally takes quite a long time. I could hardly stand up, never mind walk because the heavenly presence was so strong.

We had been Transported, Time travelled … the lady in the elevator commented, "That was quick, are we on the second floor already!" I then staggered off to lunch drunk on the heavenly bliss!

Mark Speed

On the 3rd of July, at a small local store at the co-op, there was a man in his fifties who used to live with his grandma next door to our family home. It was quite unique recognising Mark Speed. The Lord prompted me in the Spirit to recognise him. I hesitated to speak with him because I wasn't sure if I was correct about him. As I went to my car, I watched him cross over the road and walk up Heath Lane, Chester. I felt sad because he looked lonely. I jumped into my car as I had an overwhelming feeling to offer him a lift, but I didn't. I stretched out my hands, prayed for his salvation and drove away.

A few days later I received a phone call from my daughter telling me that in the newspaper there was a report of a man named "Speedy," who had been found dead in the local canal, just up the road from where I had seen him that night. It was Mark Speed. I may have been the last person to see him in this earthly realm. When I was a little girl he lived next door to us, with his grandma. We used to play with the cinders of the fireplace and the coal bunker and we played endlessly with the budgerigars in his backyard. There was a massive aviary of brightly coloured birds, green, yellow, orange and red. Prize-winning budgerigars. We got many a scolding and telling off for all our mischief-making. I believe when I prayed, he went to be with Jesus. I only wish now that I had picked him up in my car!

Martin Tuck

A few days after that I was walking the doggies one Saturday night feeling a little lonely in Chester when visiting my kids. My kids were out at a party and there was no one around that night. As I passed by down by the canal on that warm summer's evening, I saw many couples in their back gardens drinking wine and beer.

The riverfront, the pubs, married couples enjoying a glass of wine, holding hands together. Memories flooded back of spending time with my parents, husband, kids and now they were all grown up and gone. An unexpected teardrop flowed down my left cheek and I whispered in my heart, "Jesus come closer than a lover." Walking on towards the small village where I grew up as a child, I passed the bench where me and my dad sat one Sunday afternoon chewing the cud. We spoke of memories and childhood dreams, little knowing at that time that would be the last time we would sit in the warm breeze.

Distracted by these pleasant thoughts of fondness and memories of village life I stumbled upon an old friend. He was fishing, but I hardly recognised him as I hadn't seen him for many years. One of the doggies smelled fresh ham and banged her nose in the bait box he was using to catch the fish. I called out his name, "Martin! Martin Tuck!" He turned and stared as I called his name. The doggies were going wild with new smells around the fishing tackle box. Martin didn't recognise me. Larger, greying hair, laughter lines and sad lines filled his face. We made pleasantries, recalling thoughts of happier days when Rob, my children's father, worked with Martin at the electricity board and I could tell he was shocked to see me. As we talked it became apparent that he was grieving the loss of Rob, his good friend and my deceased husband, as well as the death of Martin's father and his best friend, Uncle Steve. We chatted awhile and I noticed his brown-stained fingers and cans of beer in his bag, comforting the pain.

All of a sudden Martin stood up and simply asked me for a hug. Yes, a hug! On a warm summer's evening along a tote path of a canal, Martin wept like a baby in my arms as I prayed for salvation and healing for his broken heart and many regrets.

For those of you reading this right now, expect the unexpected. Out of my own loneliness at that time in my life, the Lord brought comfort to my heart by comforting someone else. As Holy Spirit comes alongside of us, He is our comforter, our best friend.

Geranium's Fragrance

I was in Denham Springs, Louisiana in 2018 for meetings and was due to speak on the 9th of December in one of the meetings. The first night after the meeting, I went to sleep but woke in the night with the smell of geraniums. I was going to speak on frequency and sound but mainly light, but the Lord said, "I am going to download to you and you are going to speak on frequency and smell." I remembered the very fragrant geranium flowers. At the slightest breeze or the lightest touch, these plants release their perfume. I had none of my journals or books with me and was just relying on my Strong's Concordance.

Geranium seed pods resemble something called cranesbill. Some geraniums are blue, (a cornflower blue in colour). A really old- fashioned geranium has tiny purple petals.

Geranium means happiness and positive emotions. Original geraniums are usually either red, pink or white, not like hybrids which can have variegated colours. An article in the Sunday Times in 2013 said that Geraniums are plants that are near impossible to kill. They are used to make compresses to relieve pain, interestingly also used in herbal tea and this next was my favourite, they are a great housewarming gift for friendship.

The Lord showed me clearly the colours represented ruby red for the blood of Jesus, pink for His love and snow-white, like His purity.

I have enjoyed on many occasions in the heavenly realms, the presence of the fragrances of strawberries, freshly baked bread and apple blossoms.

Then He began to download *Psalm 23:5 You ¹anoint my head with fresh oil.* I love this Scripture.
Exodus 40:15 "Prophets anointed priests and kings, and the sick were anointed with oil as part of the procedure of healing by faith and by the laying on of hands."

When the stunning Holy presence swirls around you, ask yourself, "What am I smelling? Does it smell like carpenter Jesus or does it smell like the bride of Christ? Is the fragrance surrounding Him? What does our fragrance smell like?" The challenge is, the priest could not go past the holy of holies without the fragrance, the incense.

The priests went before God and they had to have the right mixture of the aroma as well as purity in their lives, or the

Lord would have smitten them.

There is a pure white Lotus lily, which symbolises the purity of your inner being. Its flower grows out of the mud and it blossoms above the muddy water. To me this has a lot of meaning that no matter what's holding you back, you can overcome it and achieve all your goals.

I did not prepare the preach. I had an hour in the morning and Kathleen Smith helped me prepare my thoughts and notes when I messaged her. I was going to preach on light and ended up preaching on fragrance.

Fragrance.
I remembered the woman who washed His feet with her tears, kissing His feet and wastefully pouring her perfume upon His feet. He told the woman who had loved much that loving Him was costly but you cannot love without giving. I only ask that this love possesses me so I may give without condition. Forgiven by Jesus.
Song of Songs 1:3 (TPT) "Your presence releases a fragrance so pleasing — over and over, poured out". (This talks about fragrant oils). (We are the fragrance of God) 2 Cor 2:15 (TPT) "We have become the unmistakable aroma of the victory of the Anointed One of God — a perfume of life to those being saved and the odour of death to those perishing".
Hosea 14:6 (NIV) "His young shoots will grow. His splendour will be like an olive tree, His fragrance like a cedar of Lebanon".
(We are like cedars — we are the perfume, fragrance and incense for medication to heal people).
Song of Songs 2:13b The budding vines of new life are now

1 To anoint means to apply oil or ointment to a person's head or body. In ancient times this was done for various reasons. Sometimes it was a sign of hospitality or of routine grooming. Those who were sick or injured were anointed with oil or ointment as medicine. But anointing was also done for sacred reasons. For example, holy anointing oil was used under the law of Moses

blooming everywhere. The fragrance of their flower's whispers, "There is change in the air".

Flowers and their oils are given to us through the trees and plants and their uses were first discovered in the Middle East, especially to help us. The Lord was showing me how myrrh and frankincense have healing properties that go well together.

There is an encounter I had on New Year's Eve with Justin Abraham and my friend Oy-chee. We had all been out and had a bit of fun in Wales. I didn't live there then but was visiting. We were sleeping in Justin's basement room but Justin, Oy-chee and I weren't ready to go to bed and were still talking in the kitchen. The kitchen at Justin's house is where so many encounters have happened and people regularly lie on the floor under the power of the Holy Spirit.

We stood chatting and I felt somebody walk up the road and up to the massive windows on the second floor of their two-story house. Preceding that, they have a massive river down the hill that flows quite fast. I often used to go to the waterfall and watch fish migrating. I felt like the person came up from the waterfall, through their big French window on the second floor and walked through the living room and into the kitchen.

As we stood there talking, I felt like the "being" walked straight through my and Oy-chee's bodies. Now we know that angels can walk through our body just as Jesus walked through the crowd. I believe the cloud of witnesses can also walk through us. I had never experienced this before and I felt the terror of God. My friend was shaking her head which she does when she experiences the Holy Spirit.

A huge electric blue eye appeared about the same height as Justin's head. Justin was still talking to us when this blue eye appeared right in front of me. It winked at me and then Justin got sucked in through the eye. I saw his whole body go in like someone slurping spaghetti. I said to Justin, "Oh my goodness! I was super scared." I did not understand the terror of the Lord like I do now. We then went to bed about six am, but I could not sleep and I hid with the covers over my head. We could see electric blue lights in the room and it felt like an angel was walking up and down the stairs of the basement. Justin told nobody for two years. It freaked us out. I knew enough in those days to know it was God. The next day we talked about it and agreed not to tell people. Justin said it had happened to him before for a whole week.

Not long after that, I had a dream and that massive blue eye appeared to me in the dream. It was to attract me to Iris Ministries and Heidi Baker. The eye sucked me into it and down a dark tunnel and there was Heidi Baker speaking to me.

Undone
by Jane Schroeder

I am in love with Him … with God.
He is always on my mind.
From the depths of my soul, I dream about Him.
Hope for mankind.

I think about Him, dream about Him.
He's always on my mind.
The Lord thinks about me, dreams about me
Because I am always on His mind.
God is in love with me.
He reveals to me His heart.
Whispering to me His mysteries of Love,
I say yes, I want to be with You Father.

You move my heart with sweet Bliss.
Piercing my very will,
My reason to live and love again.
I look up and You are there, still.

Walking in the Spirit, day by day,
In the enveloping weakness
Wearied, ravished,
Undone in Your sweet embrace of love
There's no greater comfort to be found.

You unravel my heart in love.
As You desire to be with me

Longing for the day to make all things new.
I say yes, I surrender to Your sovereignty.
I was born to be with you.
Blood transfusion.
You transform me with Your blood transfusion
Into reflections of Your light being,
A mystical union.

Luminous, radiating diamond skin.
Light being of Your love.
Breath of God dripping from honeydew lips.
In common union born above.

Every cell absorbing transforming love.
Pulsating, though my veins,
I am undone, raptured, ravished.
Beyond comprehension, in me Your Love reigns.

I am caught up into paradise,
As You play the strings of my heart.
Whether in the body or out of the body
On the Earth or in the spirit, I do not know.
In my body, or out?

All desire is to behold Your beauty.
As you call me to Your grave.
The mysterious depths of Your irresistible love.
All I desire is to behold Your beauty,
Your iridescent radiating face.

A warm, liquid tear escapes my eye,
in slow descent.
As sorrow begins to flow,

With sweet gushing blood from Your side,
My blood or yours? I do not know.

Warm, sweet, bloody bliss drips from His side.
Fresh bread, manna.
Once more the desire overwhelms me,
I surrender.

Swallowed in a golden liquid stream.
From the depths of abiding
Here, in the epicentre of Your Love,
Joy comes in!
It's a beautiful morning.

No more wearied enveloped weakness,
Look! Fresh bread, manna.
Once more, the desire overwhelms me,
I surrender.
I am in Love with Him, with God
He is always on my mind.
My Lord thinks about me, dreams about me.
Because I am always on His mind.

CHAPTER NINE
Courtrooms - Courts of the Kings and Queens

I have gained my theoretical knowledge from the learned, experienced men and women of God that I have ministered with and been around over many years, but the most important training ground has been in my personal experiences in the supernatural realms - of going intentionally, but most times unexpectedly, into these courts when dealing with different situations in my life. It all comes down to honouring Yahweh and His heavenly realms and opening up with a childlike faith to the Holy Spirit's training and the mercy and grace in the deep love of the Father to see us grow and change. I hope you enjoy my personal experiences in the realms of the Courts of Heaven.

The Chamber of Kings
A lot of the experiences that I have had are where I have either taken people to or seen them in the Chamber of Kings. There are many different levels in the Courts of Heaven, such as the Appeals Court, Angelic Court, Court of Scribes and the Court of the Kings. Lots of people go to many different places. There is one place I call the Strategy and War room. Then there is the Court of the Judges and The Sanhedrin.

Appeal Court

You go into the Appeal Court as a priest, in your priestly garments and come out as king. I seem to have bypassed a lot of other courts and have gone quickly into the Court of Kings. Ian says it is because I have mentored people. This amazed me.

I had a near-death experience in Idaho where a gas log burner was turned on to warm up a cold basement bedroom, but in the night, it was leaking gas. I remember going all night into a weird hallucinating dream. I called it "sleeping sickness" at the time.

In this state, a big tall Indian guy appeared next to my bed all night. Outside was a large raven which I knew was demonic. I now know the Indian man was Archangel Michael. He looks like a big and strong Indian or Aboriginal and doesn't seem to smile very much.

I remember dragging myself out of bed to go to the toilet wondering why I felt so bad. I undid the lids of my essential oils to see if that might help the way I felt. I Remember needing the bathroom at about 6 am and as I went out of my room, I sensed my room smelled like gas. I went up and got help from the owners. I was exhausted, but had an encounter.

Grizzly Bear Engagement

The next morning during the conference meeting I was pulled into a visionary state where I remembered taking my children to a forest in Eastham Country Park which has an old Victorian bear pit zoo which was once the home of two brown bears and their enclosure was designed to look like a cave. In the vision, the bear was angry and was chasing me and it had a large heavy choker chain around its neck which was cutting into his brown fur. I was afraid of its attack when I realised I needed to repent of all the cruelty that had taken place towards the bears. As I did this in my heart a thin golden cord encircled the bear as if it was put into a trance-like state. The chain broke off, calming this beautiful beast. Between the meeting breaks I went to Ian Clayton about this vision. He noticed a hook and a bear's claw sticking out my back. Three weeks previously while staying with my bestie, Rona Scot, I turned over in bed to feel excruciating pain in my right Teres Minor & Major Scapula muscles, which was caused by a young lady pulling me over at work while helping lift her out of her wheelchair and we thought this had caused the injury.

After the encounter the ministry team sent me to rest in the afternoon and as soon as I had lain down, I was in the Chamber of Kings which was like a promotion because I fought a bear and nearly died! In the encounter, I saw many beautiful kings and queens in beautiful gowns floating past me. None of them looked at me. The experience was visionary in black and white.

As I thanked the Lord and was so amazed that I was in there, I could see crowns. On two of the crowns was solid gold, like the king's crown. On top there was velvet. One turned from grey into beautiful emerald green and the other was red. I knew the red one was mine because that is my favourite colour. A little bit of colour started to come into the crowns and then I fell asleep.

During that evening I went to the meeting and everywhere

I went I could see the kings and queens floating past me. Ian said I had been in the Chamber of Kings.

Since then, many times I have prayed with people and seen them wearing gowns. A friend of mine I see wearing a navy velvet outfit with a green cape and a gold crown with blue velvet.

Once one of our friends took their friend into the Chamber of Kings and as she walked in, her outfit completely changed. She was wearing a blue dress with a purple robe around her shoulders. In the vision we took her out onto a balcony. It was like the pope addressing the people. When I took her hand in the physical, she was able to enter the encounter. Then I left her there. It is usually at a similar point that I leave people in the vision, having assisted them to enter their encounter. Apparently, that is what Bob Jones did, but I didn't know that he did that!

Germany
Courts of 70 Aleph Tav
I was taking one of Justin Abraham's sessions in Germany when he was sick and I was taken to a place in the Father's Kingdom called the Aleph and Tav which was like a timeline. It is the secret place of the Father where He shows us His secrets.

In the first encounter, I was taken into a courtroom. I knew this courtroom and had been before. It is called the Sanhedrin. I had looked but had never gone in before because I didn't have permission so was very surprised to have a seat there for me. In the past, I had prayed for others who were called to this courtroom. On this occasion, David Hogan was there and it was called the table of seventy. The

Hebrew letter associated with the number 70 is *Ayin*. We found out that the 70 is the court of great judgement so I was in the Court of Great Judgement, a very high place in the governmental realm in heaven.

In the centre of the Courtroom of the Sanhedrin was brilliant light with blue shards of light shooting out. It was Yeshua's body and He was spinning so fast, like a whirling white light. Lightning of communication; how we speak to each other there. The women there were all veiled and I could just see their eyes. They were Christian and were there to judge. I couldn't speak if I wanted to. It was a place to listen and learn and to go in to be judged, not to say what you want and your judgements on a situation.

Ian Clayton – Mobile, Alabama
The throne of grace is different in that the present time needs to go to Grace. Firstly, if you want something to be judged, it's best to go to the Mobile Court. Most sickness etc. have a connection to corruption and therefore need to be judged presenting ourselves to be judged. We need to be careful of going to the shadow court and getting things not from Yah's hand. We need new ways to deal with blood corruption. This comes through adoption, engaging with the record of His DNA, to be changed into His image. Changing our DNA will deal with generational stuff. Technologies are much more efficient than 1980s stuff.

On the 21st of November 2017, we were in a conference and Zion opened up. That bypassed the age of rest and age of peace. Reaching forward I pressed on to engage. We have the capacity to reach into Zion but live in the capacity of our day — the age of peace and rest are birthing chambers to something else, our future.

I am learning to become an observer of a new day so that when the day arrives, I am already living like I am on that day. I lay the right foundation tomorrow so that I will have a place to sit and the day will take care of itself.

Did you know that apostle John is one of the "Desert Fathers" on earth and in heaven, as well as being the apostle who carried the mysteries of Yahweh? The Priesthood of the mysteries of Yahweh, the realm you walk within and amongst.

When our form is changed, we will be able to materialise and dematerialise as Jesus did! John was the only disciple who put his heart and head near Jesus. It was a preparation for the Isle of
Patmos. The Revelation connected to those connected to the Earth. If we are connected to heaven, Revelation will have no reference for us. We are the only beings who can carry the presence of Yahweh woven into them.

Newbies
by Jane Schroeder

Ireland's beauty stands tall and free.
Long term friendship family.
New born babies' future kings,
David, Arthur, Judah, Atlas treasury.

Raise the Nations to former glory
Kingdoms come our legacy.
Oh fair lands of Bards and Picks,
Decree sapphire pavements destiny.

Embedded clover spread afar,
Green pastures, Celtic knots.
A white striped dream arises.
The sound of golden harps.

Come let's dance as if no one were watching,
Together let's sing as if no one were listening.

CHAPTER TEN
Russia and Germany

Stevie and I were invited to a place called Euskirchen in Germany. The festival was called "Jesus on the streets", and in our first year I took a team of five and after that, we went back every year for many years. It was a German Festival in the streets with Carnival floats and there were about twenty thousand people on the streets, people all dressed up in costumes from Gladiators to Smurfs. On the first day about forty of us in our group dressed up as Jesus, in long white robes, red sashes, shoulder-length wigs and beards, and we took a train to the main cathedral in Cologne and we would go amongst all the packed crowds and pray for people. As we were in costume as well, we fitted right into the friendly environment.

The floats came down the street with the riders throwing sweets to the spectators. There were sweets everywhere and I ate heaps but also gave a lot away and also brought some back to my friends in Wales. It was in the wintertime and this particular year it was snowing and icy when we went.

We arrived and set up a big fire tunnel, clapping in celebration of their lives and new birth in the Lord! Lots of people got saved.
The prophetic was flowing and people were given many words. It was just awesome. A brilliant place to connect. Singing, trumpets, everything. Amazing. Some were drunk

in the Spirit and some were not but they were astounded at what was happening. What was amazing about this festival was that there was no violence or shouting, just everyone was totally happy and relaxed.

We would pray for people's financial needs, healing and many prayers for businesses. Not your normal street evangelism, put it that way. It was a festival completely full of joyful singing and dancing and it was amazing.

This was going to be my first time as a speaker. I was crazy about the angelic at this time. The other speaker was someone well-known from Bethel. Our team would come together in the morning to praise and worship and then we would go out during the day on street ministry, come back to church to have a rest and eat and then usually a guest speaker would minister in the meetings at night time. We would take it in turns to speak and I spoke about the angelic. I was very green at public speaking, but just felt to talk about encounters I have had with angels. During the meeting, gold dust started to appear as my crazy Chinese friend flipped up a chair and got stuck under it. In the worship, what I call the "holy cheeky angels" show up twirling and whirling, and supernatural things started happening.

After the meeting, we went to a restaurant to eat and I had a very bad reaction to eating prawns. I got my dinner of couscous and rice and noticed these tiny pink prawns in it but had already taken a mouthful of food, and exclaimed, "Oh no prawns!" and so they quickly prayed for me and by faith I ate the rest of the meal with no reaction. I was completely healed. Previously in France, about two years

161

before, I had been prayed for after eating a prawn and had an itchy throat but no major reaction. When they prayed for me, I got completely coated in gold dust. This time no reaction at all to the prawns. I really don't like prawns that much but can eat them now and regularly eat them when I go to Indonesia.

We went back the next year to this festival and took Justin and Stevie with us and it was crazy. For some reason, we got stranded at a train station and all forty of us were jumping up and down singing the song, "Everybody Dance Now" by C+C Music Factory. There is something about dressing up as Jesus that makes you just go crazy.

I still have my Jesus costume upstairs together with the nun's outfit but I haven't worn them for very many years. People keep asking me when I will wear them again. I don't know when that time may come but I am ready just in case.

We stayed on the ground floor in a beautiful three-story house in Hanau, Germany, but I can't remember the name of the village on the edge, way out in the countryside. The weather was unusually warm and sunny for January but one morning we woke to soft powder, sugar snow. I was doing a seer school at a church for the weekend and I arrived absolutely exhausted after a crazy ten-day trip to snowy St Petersburg, Moscow.

One night while sleeping I was awakened by a vision at 2 am with helicopters flying over with SWAT teams, fully equipped, and SAS men abseiling down ropes to the ground. The helicopters were really loud and men coming down on ropes were chasing human beings that would combust into aliens in rubber suits who were body snatchers coming for human DNA. I woke up shocked and sweating. Flipping straight back into the scene again I realised that I was actually awake in another dimension.

The next morning, I woke to the beautiful smell of breakfast being prepared and went upstairs to a feast of beautiful German bread, cheese, coffee and delicious jammy doughnuts. I decided to tell no one of what had happened, as I had been up most of the night praying. I was not warfaring but sitting behind the man of war, Yahweh, who fights for me.

By the time the morning came, the Lord showed me the dream was about the Berlin Wall. I asked my host, Claudia, about this. She began to tell me a frightening story of when she was a child. Only one and a half hours away was a place called Alpha Point. The wall separated East and West Germany after the war. As a child, my host remembered the terror of crossing the Alpha Point border to visit relatives. Her dad would go to an office to get visas and she and her three siblings would sit in the car with their mother praying their family would be allowed through the checkpoint.

The Lord showed me the village where they lived was on a ley line and this was the reason it was affecting where these people lived. The couple I stayed with were both doctors and they were working on launching a complete alternative medical system. I felt like the Lord was telling me this darkness was coming against them but it would never be successful and their work would prevail. I didn't think about this dream much at the time as I was busy with the conference.

James Maloney had spoken at a conference at the church a few months earlier and deposited such a healing presence. I knew the Lord would heal spinal injuries and pain. During the service, people were shrieking and crying with joy as they came up to testify how the Lord had healed them of years of chronic pain. I believe these healings came from a deposit James Maloney had left.

It was the same in Russia. James Maloney had gone before and left a healing residue and people were getting healed. After the experience in the Courts of the Sanhedrin, I knew that when I came home from that this would be the last trip that I would do with Stevie to Germany. This was the period of time when I came to Scotland, isolated, hidden and in a loneliness like I had never felt before or even knew existed.

The sacrifices we make are nothing compared to Yahweh's. But as Katherine Kuhlman said, "A sanctified life is a lonely life." I have felt that, many times and seasons. We can romanticise the life of saints in the past but there is great sacrifice on the journey. For some saints, earthly treasure and human acknowledgement were not part of their journey. Are we truly caught up in Him being all and everything?

Would it matter if everyone walked away from us and none ever heard us preach, teach, do a miracle again? Is He enough? The journey is to question, learning the depth and joy in that new place. It can be tough for some of us when the world around us functions differently, but my prayer is that my world will have more impact than the temporary passing one. I salute all you fiery glory carriers, sold-out lovers of Him. Your journey is eternal.

Germany

After the meeting in Germany, we were taken to a beautiful massive courtyard in Germany in a place called Augsburg. We had already seen the angel over this place. We went into a room where a man used to work on Biblical scripts. A group of us prayed together and took it in stages to teach people how to look over and govern their region. Really easy. We used to do that a lot together in those days and there was an angel, Arion, holding a seven-pronged rod like a Menorah. As the staff was pointed at people's throats it began to release their voice. I knew it was Yahweh. The Fatherland of Germany returning to the Heavenly Father. It was mainly women who were getting back their voices. Because we sit in that seat above in Father's Kingdom, we govern as mothers and also as fathers. In the natural I am a widow but, in the Spirit, I rule with my Heavenly Father in the Kingdom realm.

That was when the vision ended but on the flight home, I had a second vision. Straight away I was taken into Satan's camp. It
wasn't unusual for that to happen to me as a child, which was very terrifying to me as a child but I'm not scared any more. I can see him but he can't see me. The kingdom of darkness can't see me because Satan is not in my future. In this second vision, Michael and Gabriel were also there in Satan's camp. They asked me a question with authority and grace. I felt reverence and holy fear when Michael spoke to me. He doesn't mix his words. He has a strong "no nonsense" presence about him mixed with the kindness of

Yeshua.

In Russia, A Crazy Dream

In a visionary dream state (which was grey and cloudy), the Lord said to me, "Come up here" and I knew I was in the famous Moscow Square. There was a massive procession coming through the streets in honour of people who had died. I stood high above, observing what was happening as a line of coffins was paraded past.

Crowds and crowds of people lined the street on either side, millions of people in rows. As two of the coffins came towards me in the procession, I could see right through them as if they were translucent. As I was watching, the bodies in the coffins sat up and stepped out the side of the coffins. In spite of their sin, the Lord said they were resurrecting. I knew the people in the coffins were Godly men and women from the ancient days. Now they were part of the cloud of witnesses. The dream was clear as crystal.

We read things that have gone on in history and the press can say things that aren't true but the Lord showed me that there was a history of Godly people in Russia, mystics who loved the Lord, incredible faith preachers.

Just before Christmas, we cut the album "*The Ancient Paths*", a collaboration of worship, prophetic songs and vocals with very mystical guitar music in the background carrying unusual sounds. I took it to Russia with me and some people had bought it and played it when we arrived at the retreat in Moscow.

I preached in the morning and talked about mystic and

Celtic saints. In the evening we listened to the album. I was to go around and pray for people as they lay on the floor and listened. Basically, on the album, I talk about my relationship with irresistible Jesus and how we waltz and dance together in the ballroom of His heart. The album is about ecstasy which means bliss, and it is taken from one of my favourite messages where I speak about raptures, flights of the spirit, the prayer of affection and the prayer of silence. I felt the Lord had prompted me to do a recording of this with Janine Johns.

Because I played a snippet in the morning session there was a request that we play the whole thing that evening while waiting on the Lord. As we went deeper into His presence — (It is called the ancient path and takes people into Heaven), I prayed for a few people and then sat down as I was overcome with the presence and love of God. Partway through the album we gave the interpreter a microphone to softly translate the words of the album. I then put my hand on the interpreter's wife's head to pray for her. As I prayed my hand became so heavy that I couldn't take it off. The translator saw what was going on with his wife and came and put his hand on top of my hand. With my hand still on the interpreter's wife's head I stepped back into the spirit. As I stepped back, I realised the Lord himself, in bodily form, was standing behind me. This instantly brought to mind an encounter in Coeur d'Alene, Idaho. In the worship I was turning and engaging the four faces of God, (lion, ox, eagle, man) as I sang *Yod Hey Vav Hey.*

On that occasion, I felt Ian Clayton come behind me and he said, "Let's step into The Lord together, don't be afraid." When we stepped in, Ian had disappeared and I found I was seeing out of The Lord's very eyes. This time in Russia, as I stepped back into the Lord, I was back in the beginning, in creation in Genesis Chapter 1. Wow!

As the music ended in the meeting in Russia, we decided to keep the lights turned down and people spoke about what had happened. Some could not move but others shared deeply the most unusual encounters with The Lord. The next morning the interpreter's wife could not wait to tell me her experience. She had a panoramic engagement with Jesus, walking through the heavens. We recorded it on my phone, a face time with Jesus. Lots more happened in Russia.

The Brittle Ballerina: A Short Story in Verse
by Julia Maxfield

Once upon a time
There lived a Russian ballerina.
She grew up estranged
From her native ancestral forest -
Taken at an early age
From her arching palace
Of slender silver birches
And fairy-tale silvan imaginings
Cultivated in the nutritious dark soil
Of mother folklore -
And, like a potted plant, displaced.
Her red cloak of riding hood
Having been torn by wolves,
She was sold into captivity.
She lived in the metropolis,
Where her indigenous song could not be.
The towering scapes of buildings
Took her breath away:
Crisp geometric planes
Of soaring public spaces
Conceived by the people, for the people
Whilst not exactly noble,
Yet were quickened by
The pulse of revolutionary thought -
Dawn of a scientific era un-daunted
No longer haunted by the past,
A time of enlightened architectural change.

She became fluent
In the languages of various
Interlocking subcultures:
She could survive in them all.
She graced the narrow social circles
Of aristocratic bohemians,
Attending dinner parties
Where the small talk
Still revolved around art,
Still breathed the elegant romance
Of a nineteenth-century novel
In all its detailed minutiae,
Updated and urban-chic;
Where the silvery dinner plates
Still reflected angels
In the frescoed ceilings -
Airy imitations of Tintoretto,
And the like.
Or, she descended
Into an underworld of nightclubs
And of glimmering, Cimmerian wit -
Drinking vodka on the rocks
With her hipster friends
To lose hated inhibitions
Under pretence of irony -
Watching pole dancers
Become miner's canaries,
Expressive of a garish desperation
To be seen and heard -
Accidentally baring their souls
As they bared their bodies
To a pinstriped, jetlagged audience
Of dissociated business men.

Ruthlessly, she
Perfected her own art.
She grew absorbed
In her personal hall
Of full-length mirrors,
High barres and polished floors -
Shuttered and enclosed
By internal revolving doors
Accentuating the confirmation bias
Of her carefully-chosen surroundings.
Her staccato steps were increasingly Successful:
By many suitors and artistic connoisseurs
Who idolised the nuances
Of her grand-pliés and demi-tours,
Was she greatly adored.
Men's egos she crushed like ice -
Self-conscious yet unaware,
She subjugated her own pain
Until it became a jagged weapon
Casually impaling others
In the endless turmoil of heartbreak.
And subtly,
She drew would-be critics
To conform to the vanity
Of her ephemeral wishes -
Not realising her own conformity
To something that was grey and sad
As hardened smoke.
Caged in the unreal city,
She was forever taking flight
And never free.
Until one day in January,
Month of the two-headed

171

Roman god Janus
And the open door,
The unthinkable happened.
A miracle took place
Beside the frozen lake
Where children had not skated
For decades.
Watching an ancient swan's
Foolish attempts
To clamber, again and again,
Into a boat moored in the rushes,
She experienced, in the agony
Of its silent struggle,
A dreamwhite epiphany:
Something closer to artistic truth
Than the svelte pose
Of a dancer's bare arms.
Then did the icy waters break
Shattering the hall of mirrors
Held in infinite regress.
No longer would she perform
Like Clara at cocktail parties
Before a shadow prince
With devouring nutcracker jaws.
Crystal-clear, instead she saw
The whole optical illusion
Subside and collapse -
Columns of glittering chandeliers
Rows of tinkling music boxes
Dolls of descending size
Confetti sprays of genius
Hollow sculptures adorning banquets
Kaleidoscopic spiral stairs -

The entire swirling hologram receded,
Washed away like Noah's flood.
A tabula rasa Is all that was left
At that point of stillness:
An empty, virgin slate.
And so to Africa she came
In order to begin again
By teaching dancing
In a school for orphans -
Bequeathing charity,
The gift of love,
In a land of yellow savannah,
Golden sun.
There, she heard the tale
Of her origins,
Re-awakened and re-told
By storybook animals:
Loping giraffes with gracious necks
And sweeping eyelashes
Revealed new rhythms and
Inspired fresh forms.
She found solid comfort
In maternal pairs of arms
Whose mutely generous embrace
Said more than any language
She had ever learned before.
She was hungry for their food:
She learned how to savour
Slow stew's magical warmth.
She learned how to sit and wait
With spry old men
Selling green bananas
In the red roadside dust.

173

No longer Atalanta,
The swift-footed goddess forever
Outdistancing
Legendary golden apples,
She discovered how to stop -
And, with clumsy bare-handed patience,
Remove the worms
From an elderly woman's feet.
No longer spell-bound,
She was finally free
To receive the riches of the poor.
However,
It was from the children
Whom she came to teach
That she learned the most.
Through them she met
A radiant man in white:
Who said to the deaf and dumb
Parts of her, with softly creative breath,
"Ephphatha, Be Open!"
The children's songs of praise
To the resurrected God-man
Seemed to emanate from a light world
Somewhere remotely near -
Each syllable, in the divine shape
Of their transfigured native tongue,
Descended as a perfect gift.
They wept when she wept,
Their faces starred with tears -
Yet she encountered joy
Through the trustful rainbows
Of their smiling eyes
That saw her unclouded and innocent,

As if for the first time.
She found herself naked,
Stripped bare and utterly defenceless
In the presence of pure Love.
Now, in humility she wields
The precision of her artistic gifts
As a sword -
Not to destroy others, but to liberate -
Teaching many how to find
Their unique dance steps,
In her boldness a lioness
Who knows her value
And fully understands the cost
Of the trials that have been
And those yet to come.
For she has chosen
To make this journey to the end -
Knowing that all those who inherit
The kingdom of heaven
Are childlike and poor in spirit,
And they shall live

CHAPTER ELEVEN

The Beginning of the Celtic Journey

I ask, can we unravel certain parts of history soaked in the saints' and martyr's blood, when it has paved the way for our own scrolls in life? Mingled in with Christ's blood, as He has already seen it all and paid for it all. The echo sound of songs across hills and valleys, and vibrations of the movement of His Holy Spirit across earth and time, the merging light of His glory uniting us with those of ancient paths and ancient days. Inseparable, over time, unified IN the ONE body flowing in light, sound, colour — of His Blood! Now they watch, wait and cheer as we carry on the journey, the path of remembrance, revitalisation and revelation. These stories bring us closer to the past than we would have believed and encourage us that even when days seem dark in current times, nothing can hold us down as we step into the Glory of God.

Iona of Scotland

Scripture Isaiah 6:1 "I saw also the Lord sitting upon the throne (in Scotland) high and lifted up. And his train filled the temple. And the Lord showed me his train or robe was the robe of righteousness".

Scotland Ablaze; a small gathering of people in Stevie's house in St Michael's Whyd, Kilwinning. An accomplished keyboard player, Graham Mcneil was flowing in the heavenly presence while Stevie lay on the floor quietly repeating over and over again as he wept; Jesus, Jesus, Jesus!

I heard a humming sound like a children's humming top, with a whoosh, whoosh, whoosh. We were singing backwards and
forwards about Jesus and I heard an audible voice and I felt to look up. As I looked the heavenly dimensions split open like a curtain drawn back in front of my eyes and I was seeing my Lord God's feet up to His knees. Shimmering, shining light, radiating, illuminating, white light, the rest of His bodily form was a silhouette.

I was looking at a forty-degree angle and the Lord was there on a massive, huge throne. I heard the throne before I saw it and I
could see right up to God's knees. At first, I thought it was an angel because the rest of His outline was pure white light. My body was shaking from the inside out, trembling. The Lord, His feet, knees and His throne seemed to be slightly above my head. It was so close I could almost touch it. At the back of the throne, there was fabric, a bit like silk or foil. It was a living, moving, frequency fabric, like streams of rivers, alive and dancing. It was living purple. I know purple often signifies kingly royalty. This ribbon fabric began to fill every part of Stevie's house, the plug sockets, every crack in the wall, beneath the ground, in the foundations and above. I asked the Lord what was happening and He said "Iona has moved to Kilwinning."

In the Abbey on Iona, I sat on one of the pews. I fell asleep in a vision state. I saw the Abbey on Iona being dismantled one brick at a time, being rebuilt in Ayrshire, Scotland, being built one brick at a time. It's talking about the governmental anointing of Saint Columba and the saints had been moved and rebuilt in Ayrshire.

Sunday morning, I was running past Stevie's mum and dad's house. I stopped and there was no roof on their house and the Lord said, "This house will be known as the start of revival in Kilwinning."

Scottish Beach Walks

So, I walk beaches every day with rain, hail and blasting gale-force winds. I nearly got blown into the sea one day, but shouldn't have gone out in 60 km gale-force winds. One time I cried my eyes out on the beach, wondering what I was doing in this God-forsaken place and then repented because God has not forsaken Scotland at all! Then we decided I would have the family dogs to keep me company more and that is when Millie and Eva came to live with me three weeks of every month.

One windy walk on the beach on my own, someone came next to me and held my hand. There was Jesus holding my hand, in bodily form, walking with me along the beach in His hot, and sandy desert feet. Even though it was really cold here on the beaches of Scotland, we were walking in a different dimension and it felt warm and calm and at the same time behind that the loud wail of creation groaning for the Sons of God to be revealed.

I don't know how long we walked. We didn't talk, I just kept looking at His feet because it was peaceful, warm and comforting. This made me realise that I couldn't remember the last time I had spoken with Holy Spirit who comes beside me. I lost track of time and began to remember who I am, what I am and why I am here. Living in Scotland you can have four seasons in one day, three or four times a day. It can be sunny, blasting rain and the wind will drop, all in twenty minutes.

Poem
by M.M. van Rensburg

it is late spring in my Scottish garden
an enclosure, with a gate and then a field
in this garden is a shrub; it grows out of the wall
it has green leaves and white blossoms with four petals on
it
they seem to burst out from twenty-two yellow-green
tentacles
i did not plant them
i just watered the bare branches
but now
here they are triumphant in my garden
but if this was not enough
the lingering sublime beauty balance
of these mystical blossoms in my secret garden
linger in my mind
not only with their cleansing angelic white leaves
but the smell, oh the smell
a smell so smoky and pure
a smell that pulls me upwards
a smell that jerks my right side
and flows through my being
singing sweet songs of a place, i have been before
a place where my soul longs to return

Stevie and I in Glasgow, 5th January 2019

Stevie and I drove forty-five minutes into the centre of Glasgow to a big old-fashioned church with a massive pillar. It was the church of a famous revivalist and we went to this church last night, where the revivalist's daughter, Grace, was speaking. The meeting and building seemed really old fashioned and the ladies were sitting in the front of the church praying in turn prior to the start of the service. As I sat down, I felt the presence which I now understand to be the presence of the Lord. An elderly lady got up as the MC announced that we would sing a hymn and as we sang, the presence fell. Stevie said he experienced the cloud of the Lord the whole time, but I didn't see it. We would sit and stand with the hymns and prayers, shared straight from the hearts of the people. It was the strangest thing that happened twice in the service - as I closed my eyes, and even though it was black when my eyes were closed, a shadow passed past my eyes. Then they spoke about being overshadowed by God. I was undone!

A man sat next to me on a pew singing old hymns. Reality kicked in; it was my dad coming in the spirit to sing with us. As a child, we children would all sit sedately and sing songs of praise from a TV program on Sunday nights. As a youth leader, my dad would sometimes take the services in the Methodist church. My beloved dad died in the August of 2015. He loved life, he loved creation, he loved so much I am sure he's tending the gardens in heaven. I still miss him dearly. We used to garden together. Funnily enough yesterday was the first time I had dug in the garden of my new home and that night was when his presence was with me at the meeting for a little while.

Grace spoke about the baptism of Holy Spirit. We cried out for God to come again in power and fire. We sang about five hymns in one go and people came to the front to rededicate their lives to the Lord. The fear of the Lord descended. Apparently, that is what the function of this church is — "The fear of the Lord and revival!"

I couldn't get out of my seat to get to the front even though I wanted to because the presence of the Lord was so strong. It was beautiful. I just wanted to go to that church again and again.

It was packed out. Every pew was full. There must have been well over two hundred people. They meet every Saturday night and have children's work. All I can say is — the cloud and the fear of the Lord — overshadowed by God himself. Probably the best night's sleep I have had in ages!

June 2017
Ireland of the Celts
Quote From "Restoring The Woven Cords", strands of Celtic Christianity for the church today. by Michael Mitton.
Brigid was born at Faughart near Dundalk, Louth, Ireland in 450 AD. Her father was Dubhthach, an Irish chieftain or King of Leinster and her mother, Broisseach (Brocca) was a Christian Pict slave. Dubhthach's wife forced him to sell Brigid's mother to a Druid priest when she was pregnant. However, some time upon meeting St. Patrick, she was apparently baptised by Patrick who discerned the call of God on her life. Some years later the King decided to have his daughter back in the palace.

The local Chief refused to give Brigid a small plot of land. Characteristically Brigid persevered, eventually getting him to agree to give her a piece of land no bigger than the size of her cloak. Brigid laid down her cloak on the grass where it grew and covered the whole of Curragh, thus one of the most famous communities.

Kildare (Cill Dara — meaning Church of the Oak) was famed for its magical oak trees, very special to the Druids.

Brigid's community turned it into a centre where Christ was exalted and the light of the Gospel shone from this community to the pagan world around it. She lit a fire at the centre of the community as a sign of this light. Only women were allowed to tend the fire, which remained alight for a thousand years, until the dissolution of the monasteries.

A fundamental difference between Celtic societies and other European societies is that the female had a unique place of prominence and was regarded equally and could even be elected chief, leader of her TRIBE!

Icenian Boudicea (also known as Boudicea in Latin and Buddug in Welsh) was queen of the British Iceni tribe and in 60AD led as a military commander while her Roman sisters could not own property. Effectively, when a woman married, she and all her belongings belonged by law to her husband's family, whereas a Celtic woman continued personally to own all she brought into the marriage with her husband. He had no rights over her property.

The Tribe was a close-knit family and an interesting feature of Pictish institutions was inheritance through the female. Both parents took responsibility and both parents were free to follow their work, leaving the children safely in the care of the Tribe. Brigid, Hilda, Ebba, Ethelburga and others held leadership roles in their communities. The rights of women didn't seem to have been an issue. Respect and acceptance like Brigid showed the origination abilities, energy and common sense of Teresa of Avila.

A legendary tale which suggests that there would have been some who were very comfortable with the idea of Brigid being a priest and bishop. William Parker Marsh recorded a story of her visit with other women to Telcha Mide "taking the veil" led by Bishop Mel! A fiery pillar rose from her head to the roof ridge of the church. Then said Bishop Mel: "Come, O holy Brigid, that a veil may be sained (to make the sign of the cross) on thy head before the other virgins."

It came to pass then, through the grace of the Holy Ghost that the form of ordaining a Bishop was read over Brigid. Mac Caille said that a bishop's order should not be conferred on a woman. Said Bishop Mel, "No power do we have in this matter that dignity hath been given by God onto Brigid, beyond every woman." Wherefore the men of Ireland from that time to this give episcopal honour to Brigid's successor.

CHAPTER TWELVE
Shin and the Holy Fire

Elephant, Mildura 2019

So much more important is the love of God folded up inside of us. Interestingly, I've been preaching about the different facets of love all year. Facet, what a fabulous descriptive word this is. It means; *A particular aspect or feature of something. (Aspect, feature, side, dimension, characteristic). One side of something many-sided, especially of a cut gem. (Surface, face, side, angle)*

Elephant

Six years ago, on a flight to Germany, on a European trip, the plane achieved its elevation and as I looked out of the window, I had a vision. There was a big eye filling the window. At first, I thought I was in the deep sea and it was the eye of a whale. At the time I was living in Wales and thought the whale might be related to where I was living. As I looked deeper asking Papa God, I realised it was an old Indian elephant's eye which had come into view.

Recently, I flew into Melbourne, Australia, and I felt to watch the children's movie "Dumbo the Elephant." The movie reminded me of the vision of the elephant's eye from six years before and I found myself sucked into that same vision, but this time the impression was stronger.

The film was about the bond between the elephant baby

and his mum, and even when they were separated, they were connected with their thoughts and intents of their hearts. This reminded me strongly of the bond between human mother and child and the bond that exists between us and our Papa God. Some might call it an open heart, which is a sensing, feeling and seeing heart. This is called Cardiognosis, knowledge of the heart in a metaphysical sense. Heart talk or telepathic awareness, the thoughts and intents of the heart communicated without words to those we love. It's often known as the supernatural gift of Cardiognosis led by Saints who received it, to establish in their heart an inner dialogue, an inner knowledge of God.

I call it the "Awe Spark of Yahweh," the umbilical DNA between me and my Father. On occasions, I see in the Spirit an electric blue lightning strand coming out of my belly, like a twirling, twisted DNA ladder. In Heaven it is like a convergence of lightning shots around the Father but instead of going down to the Earth, it is like a carousel connecting my heavenly body with God. This "Awe-spark of Yahweh" is my personal communication with the "Three in One."

I see it as if our fluid goes up our spinal cord, that is the waters above seen in Genesis 1. The Hebrew letter for water is "*mem*", the memory water. The memory amniotic fluid vibrates and that is how He speaks to me. Sometimes it is a whoo, whoo, whoo, whoo, whoo sound and sometimes it is more like a humming groan deep within my being.

Jesus would kiss me on the lips a lot and I began to realise it was all about morphing into Him in the oneness. Eye to eye, mouth to mouth, heart to heart in an entwining love tapestry, a lover's embrace. The waltz, two dancers moving together in circles. The music was purposely written for that sort of dance, "The Waltz" performed primarily in a closed position.

The Elephant Never Forgets.

Elephants are family oriented; they are giant beasts. Very attentive to their young, very strong leaders. They all go to the watering hole together as a herd. They represent strength, honour, stability, patience, longevity, stamina and long life. It is believed that an elephant's trunk could also represent wisdom.

The Hebrew word *Shin* (pronounced Sheen) has a meaning of "teeth." The elephant has very big ivory tusks. The word elephant is not found in scripture except indirectly. In the original Greek word "elephantinos" is translated "of ivory." (Revelation 18:12). The Hebrew word *Shenhabin* has a meaning of "tooth rendered ivory."

I Kings 10:22 (NASB)
22 For the king had at sea the ships of Tarshish with the ships of Hiram; once every three years the ships of Tarshish came bringing gold and silver, ivory, apes and peacocks.
2 Chronicles 9:21(NASB)
21 For the king had ships which went to Tarshish with the servants of Hiram; once every three years the ships of Tarshish came bringing gold and silver, ivory, apes and peacocks.

The elephant represents the ancient script keepers because they live so long. They hold the scrolls and scripts of their nations and their peoples. I could expand on this but at this time these are my thoughts.

Elephant Funerals

As elephants travel across the forests and open land, they remember the ground where other elephants have died. They stop in the very spot where the bone remains of the dead elephants lay or are even buried, stomping the ground and raising their trunks to trumpet.

They will then spend days at the burial site of the remains, covering the remains with leaves. The herd will go off to the water holes and come back day after day grieving for the lost elephant, even when it is not part of their herd family.

I see such a connection between the Hebrew letter *Shin* and the matriarchal elephant because the *Shin* is seen in the spirit as a matriarch, a woman who is head of her family or tribe, an older woman who is powerful within a family or organisation. The *Shin* has also been seen in visions and dreams, massively colourful, and decorated like an Indian elephant with bright red and gold. I believe this bright, brilliant, shiny red and gold colour represents the marriage, the wedding ring, and the circle of love with Father, Son and the Holy Spirit.

The *Shin* is the first living letter that stepped out to me in a pillar of fire, mirroring the Lord putting His very Spirit within me. His living, active, moving, very Spirit within all of us. We are a beautiful, luminous, radiant, shiny reflection of Yahweh. [1]The *Shin* is the tooth; it means sharp, press, to be pierced, to sharpen. It means to lay hold and not let go.

The early Semitic/Hebrew of Shin ‭ש‬ is a tooth. I think it looks more like a back molar than front teeth. The Hebrew word *shān* means tooth (Strong's H8127). It is from the root word *shä-nan'* which means "sharpen, prick, to teach diligently", (Strong's H8150). *Psalm 45:5 "The arrows are sharp. The people fall under you. Your arrows are in the heart of the King's enemies."*

The *Shin* is not only a flame of fire or sharp teeth but holds onto the promises that the *Shin* also represents the crowns, hence the name the Lord gave me of "Fiery Crown and Glory."

The *Shin* brings us face-to-face with El Shaddai. I believe this is the total purpose of why the living letters are stepping out to me
Isaiah 41:15 (The Voice) "I will turn you into a formidable threshing sledge with brand new blades that will mow down entire mountains and turn the hills into chaff."

[1]The four-headed *Shin* is on the back of the tefillin and is concealed from view. It represents the world to come or that which is not presently seen. It is the belief that the *Shin* also represents the four desert mothers, Sarah, Rebecca, Leah and Rachael.

How fascinating is that? The mother side of Yahweh and His four desert mothers brought to bear, bringing to birth in the world to come. Amen.

Holy, Holy, Holy - Esh Oklah, God is a Consuming Fire
God sometimes manifests Himself through images of fire, as a blazing torch, a pillar of fire or even a burning bush. In the Hebraic language *Esh Oklah,* (AISH O-KLAH) God is a consuming fire, a jealous God for our total affections, we are His beautiful obsession, a target for His bull's eye love.

189

He has been reminding me of late that He wants to be our fiery passion to bring us into the devouring embers of His presence and loving embrace. One of the meanings of the Hebrew letter *"Shin,"* is the terror of God Himself.

During this time of engagement and encounter with the Living
Letter, *Shin*, a man's head appeared amongst the orange-yellow burning, moving flames and I heard a voice say, "Run into the fire, don't shy away, run into the fire! I AM will change you by fire!" *Exodus 3:2 (NASB) The angel of the Lord appeared to him, (Moses) in a blazing fire from the midst of a bush; and he looked, and behold, the bush was burning with fire, yet the bush was not consumed.*

The realisation was that the Lord Himself had appeared to me in the flames, to show us that we are the messengers of His face, with no veil between us, unbridled, glorious habitation, face to face encounter in the Kingdom realms, resulting in us becoming one with His living, breathing breath, the oracles of His mysteries. The House of one, the *Aleph — Beyt* House of perfection.

I was allowed to see many people that day in the meeting embrace the burning heart of a love sacrifice unto God. The invitation still stands today, to be the reflection of His love and grace, Papa God occupying the house when people look upon our faces! I believe this Spiritual encounter was for a reason and a purpose for the Ecclesia, the body of

---

1 The Hebrew definition of the Shin described by Elizabeth R. Corley, quoted from "Friends of Eber, Scrolls of Zebulon". Also, see page 40 in this book for the reference to the Hebrew word "Shin".

1 The three-headed Shin is featured in the tefillin, the box worn on the foreheads of the orthodox Jews. The three-headed Shin faces people and represents the world as it is now. It also represents the three desert fathers, Abraham, Isaac and Jacob.

Christ at that time, as we were just beginning to learn the Hebrew *alefbet* and *ivri* through the amazing teachings and impartations of Karl Whitehead's living active encounter realms around his life.

Diary 15th November 2012.

I am starting to go back now. It is quite freaky. The Lord spoke to me clearly and said look up *Ezekiel 37:4-8* where the Lord prophesied to the dry bones.

I felt a tingling feeling all around my mouth and I began crying, birthing and travailing. The Lord spoke to me again (in those days I didn't understand the Lord speaks in your heart but at that time I just heard it in my head). The Lord said, "You will speak life and a double-edged sword will come out of your mouth." This was in 2012 and He said, "You will go to dry places and speak forth My words of life. Don't worry what to say or what to wear. Some places you will wear sackcloth and be hidden and then revealed. Don't look to the right or the left, just look straight ahead to Me." We went to some very dry places and did speak to the land and the people in a very hidden way.

This is a quote the Lord gave me and it must have been when Ian first came to the UK over eight years ago.
Jane: "I believe in the next phase we will experience God's power like never before. This will be a new level of God's fiery presence and healing."

Isn't it wacky that this is starting to happen now on my last trip! This is the start of a new healing movement with miracles, signs and wonders and you guessed it, what

1Quote by Teresa Bowen from the amazing book "Friends of Eber" Scrolls of Zebulon publications.

we just spoke about, deeper revelation. Isn't it awesome looking back and finding what you wrote and seeing it starting to manifest?

On the 20th of October 2012, I woke up repenting of a lack of love for people, (I needed to do that a bit more then). The quote I read when I woke up to this, is by Daniel Black. Daniel says, "Everything we do, if for His own sake, that He may receive all the love that is fully due to Him." I didn't really know Him all that well then. There is nothing greater than to lie down and wrap myself in Him and to lavish all the oil of my love upon Him. The Lord was speaking to me saying the more I love Him the more I will love people.

Song of Songs 8:6-7 (TPT)
6 Fasten me upon your heart as a seal of fire forevermore.
This living, consuming flame
will seal you as my prisoner of love.
My passion is stronger
than the chains of death and the grave, all-consuming as the very
flashes of fire from the burning heart of God.
Place this fierce, unrelenting fire over your entire being.
7 Rivers of pain and persecution will never extinguish this flame.
Endless floods will be unable
to quench this raging fire that burns within you. Everything will
be consumed.
It will stop at nothing
as you yield everything to this furious fire
until it won't even seem to you like a sacrifice anymore.

Flame of His Name
by Jane Schroeder and Janine John

The one with the fiery heart consumes us with His love,
The one with the fiery heart pursues us with your love,
Faith, Hope, Love, the greatest of these is Love.
With a fiery heart You burn, with fiery heart You yearn.
We were born from above,
You encircle me, in a never ending ring of love,
Encircled, madly in love with us in a dream of dreams.
Ecstatic love, as I get caught up in you, ecstatic love,
We have positioned ourselves in your heart,
Singing heart of fiery love,
It's a love flame, you're a love flame.
Golden Tower of His name, liquid love.
Golden Strands of His voice wrapped up inside His voice.
The interlocking crown of His name of His flame.
Born from the first voice, the voice of Thunder.
I was born from above, was born from your love.
I was born from a dream, a song of the king.
I was born in Zion with the song of a wing over me.
I have always known your flame, always known your fame.
I was born out of the burning heart of the flame of your
name.
I remember the sound His voice,
many waters making me brand new,

Original design, all the sounds of God.
I was born in wonder,
I was born in all the Thunder of Him,

I remember the fire, the light of Him.
I was in His heart the heart of a King.
I sit at the table of legacy.
Framed up all around all the time, the Government of God,
I sit at the table of legacy.
I was born in awe and wonder,
I was born in all the thunder;
I remember the fire, the light of Him.
I was in His heart the heart of a King.
Rooted in His empowering love, His great affections.

In closing, I would like to share two stories to inspire and encourage us all.

Ancient Way!

We are presently in an age that calls for revolutionaries. Systems require complete overhauls, complete recreation. First, the church. As the church goes, so goes the world. I have heard the Lord speak to me about the "new and ancient way" for so many years, but I keep hearing it.

We need revolutionaries to rise up with the wisdom of the "new and ancient way." Courageous in the face of opposition, stagnation, and religion. Convinced of their position and unflinching in the face of intimidation and accusation. We are about to see the dawn of the age of the revolutionary. They will be oracles and they will not waver in truth. They are creatives, living from the heart of the great Creator.

Undaunted. Sure. Convinced. Prepared to give all. They will stand and sing the songs of revolution. They will run and not grow weary; they will walk and not faint. They will live in peace of union with Christ and nothing else will matter to them but His Heart, and they will release justice like we've not yet seen before from the church in our day.

Get ready. The revolutionaries are rising and things are about to change. Stand by the roads, and look for the ancient paths, where the good way is; and walk in it; and find rest for your souls." *Jeremiah 43:18-19 (NIV) "Forget the former things; do not dwell on the past. See I am doing a new thing! Now it springs up; do you not perceive it? I am making a way in the wilderness and streams in the wasteland".*

So, I would like to finish off with the following story of a very dear friend of mine who leads by example. You don't have to be famous, brilliant at many things, and intellectual, a scientist, a professional sportsperson, design a great invention (although all of these things and people matter in the plan of life), you really need to just be yourself and do the "thing" that Yahweh purposed and planned for you before the beginning of time. Be yourself!

A Most Beautiful Lady!
(Names have been changed in this story to protect the privacy of those in the story).

There was this beautiful girl (Alison) who gave birth to a son (Noah). She showed up in this Baptist Church in Manchester for prayer. One of my friends gathered "strays" from all over the world and she's a lady who I met when I was a mobile hairdresser and used to go to all different people's houses to do their hair.

We began to get to know Alison really well and began to

love her! She lived in some Council flats and was often in very dire places. She then met this beautiful guy from church, who funnily enough lived down the road from us in Chester. Alison and this guy got married. Sam, my son grew up with Noah and they began to do all different things together to do with church. Noah had sleepovers at our house. He began to go very, very thin and I was worried that he might be on drugs or drinking meths. We had this great big park in our area and I had to drag some teenagers out of there in the middle of the night. They would be drinking gin in the park with these crazy drug dealers. At this stage, Noah seemed to disappear and we lost contact with him.

So, Alison gave birth to another little boy (Daniel), oh he was beautiful! Life went on and this little family were in a really great church and were doing really well. Unfortunately, eventually, the marriage broke down. It was really sad. Alison moved out and she met this other guy, (Stephen) who was a local Entrepreneur and the nicest guy that she had met yet. He was a money lender and they lived above this Café. Her background was that she was a very damaged lady who went on to have two daughters by Stephen. He absolutely adores these daughters still to this day.

There was a big TV report about where they were running a charity and it was a scam. To this day Alison says that they weren't and they were innocent, but they were investigated and it came out that it was so. Alison was a very shy, quiet lady, but she was a magnet, a total evangelist. Everywhere she would go, people would give their lives to Jesus, but she was used and abused by Christians. She lived in some of the most deprived places in Chester, a place called Blacon.

I would visit her there, and at the time her youngest daughter was about six years of age and Alison had this lady who was on drugs, in and out of prison living with them and she was in the local church. Alison was amazing. When the Café closed, because someone else did her in financially, she just took it over and ran it. Rona and I would worry about her a lot. She still comes to us for prayer even now if there is a situation, but things have shifted a lot for her recently.

Alison and her family had little corn snakes, rats, mice, dogs, cats and all sorts in their house. All the snakes used to scare me silly.

One day I was doing her mum's hair and her mum would have all these fabulous colours like pink hair, green hair — she had beautiful blond hair and she was just so beautiful and innocent. I was doing her mum's hair, which would take me hours, painting these coloured streaks in her hair and she would always have loads of people popping in and out of the house. Ninety per cent of the time I didn't get paid for doing her hair because they didn't have the money for it, but I would just get paid for the products.

I didn't mind though as I just loved on them and loved doing it for them. My Ruthie was fourteen at the time and could tell you some amazing stories as well.

There was a Morning Star Conference and Alison was part of that and everywhere she went, people would get healed. I stayed with her for the time of this conference and in her house were all these snakes, creatures and animals. Alison would never push herself forward, but they did write a book about her. Stephen, her former husband and her became best of friends even though they had split up and he had half of the children and her the other two. The children have all grown up to be absolutely gorgeous people. One has had a grand baby, one is in the army but Noah, at twenty-one, who lived down the road from us, hung himself.

We could not believe it. Sam was just devastated and Sam and his girlfriend at the time went through a stage where lots of people they knew either tried to or did commit suicide. In Sam's dad's house, they were renting out some of the rooms to help pay for the mortgage and this girl was away on holiday and the guy was with his parents, and this black snake-like thing, like a wiggly worm was in the house and the Lord showed me that the girl tried to commit suicide in the house. I asked my family and they didn't want to tell me, and I said that they should have done so straight away.

Alison is brilliant now. She went back to live with her mum for a while, changed her job situation where she was being bullied at work. She is now married again with a baby and things have turned out really well from the beginning of some really difficult situations to where things are fine now and all because of the power of prayer, coming before the Lord and bringing them before Him and holding them in our hearts.

So, Alison happened to come to a meeting with this massive speaker, a lady from the USA, called Christine Ford. What an incredible woman, known for her prophecies who runs a church and is now opening a School of Ministry. Christine came and we had this beautiful open house and I hosted her for three days in Chester. Man did they work her hard at those meetings. The leader of the meetings would go home tired and we would be left with loads of people getting prophecies, but one that stood out, we had her all to ourselves in my beautiful friend's country house lounge. Alison was there, and we were praying for a team that runs the church, helps the church and comes to the church. Christine gave some really amazingly crazy prophecies somewhere off the scale. She said to Alison, "You're the Queen, you are the queen and I see you in the future living in your palace," and Alison was like, "I believe it!" She believed like blindly and innocently, not childish, because she's had a really difficult life and had to push through, but with childlike faith. We were all like — yeah bring it! But that was the total opposite of where she was at, at that time in her life.

Later on, in time, Alison got offered this absolutely beautiful country house on the outskirts of Chester in a posh place called Mollington. She opened up afternoon teas there with little meeting rooms where people could come and hire the rooms.
She was a whiz at it. She painted out, with the person that owned it, all the upstairs bedrooms and named them Noah, Moses and Elisha, all different rooms. I stayed in one of the rooms; it was fantastic and the breakfasts were spectacular. She turned that place around, even doing weddings and baby showers, and finally they were doing so well. We even had my daughter's baby shower there. We just paid for the food and the room was free.

Finally, she met her dream husband, they got married and Alison took on his daughter and it was amazing until they got a notice from the person who owned this beautiful building and said they were going to sell it! They didn't give her an option to buy it, rent it, nothing. Alison coped really well but her husband was not impressed with Christians. He was sort of a nominal Christian and he really struggled, so he said, "I'm leaving," and left Alison holding the "baby" in a sense. She had lots of people to help her through this season. He went off and bought a house with some of the profits they had made in another place that was pretty rough, called Elton. The Post office next door was closing down so they asked him if he wanted it to use and he wouldn't have to pay any rent on it. Alison turned it into the most beautiful Café design, serving green teas. They also bought this crazy little takeaway and they started doing breakfasts and during Covid, they sold afternoon teas that they delivered with this beautiful little Mini car. She named the restaurant (Queen's Palace Place Country House), the "Little Molly-Mollington."

There was a big posh hotel across the road which was the big "Mollington" and then there were these small office units and Architect's building. People always called the place "Mollington," therefore — "Little Molly" and it was booming and of course already people wanted to steal it off her AGAIN! This time she contacted Rona and I and we started praying and it was doing really successfully and then she got offered a job, a job! Her dream job! The word became flesh and dwelt amongst her and all good things come to those who come before the Lord and wait on Him and be kind to one another and love one another.

Even the poorest of the poor, the criminals, the murderers where she lived. She so mentored people, and is known in heaven as a "Mother Teresa" of Chester, she is incredible.

So, I finish by saying, "Guys, keep in that place of faith, great faith — Faith is a being, Faith is an angel, Faith is a canopy like a cloud that comes around you, and folds like the wind of the Lord and is your strong tower of the Lord that you run into and are safe. Faith is the substance of things that you hope for and things to come. So, I bless you.

OVERWHELMED the Poetry Book

A book of inspirational poems of my deep personal encounters and intimate journey with God. Forged from strolling the beaches, connecting with the land, honouring creation — once walked by our ancient forefathers.

ABOUT the Author

Jane Schroeder currently resides in wee bonny Scotland in the UK, and is the founder of Nun On The Run, Fiery Crown And Glory. com and Woven Colours. Fueled by her passion and desire for others to know God's love, and as well as ministering around the world, she is a businesswoman and constantly expands her personal boundaries learning new skills and things. She shares with a passionate heart and love to equip, desire and see Sons and Daughters arise into their original intent of Kingship, the dimensions of Heaven and eternal bliss.

SeraphCreative

Heaven's Heart for Earth

Seraph Creative is a collective of artists, writers, theologians & illustrators who desire to see the body of Christ grow into full maturity, walking in their inheritance as Sons of God on the Earth.

Sign up to our newsletter to know about future exciting releases.

Visit our website :

www.seraphcreative.org